I0225126

STAYING TOO
LATE
LEAVING TOO
SOON

TRICKS ✛ TRAPS ✛ TRUTHS OF RELATIONSHIPS

TIM GRIER

Published By:
Jasher Press & Co.
www.jasherpress.com
customerservice@jasherpress.com
1.888.220.2068
P.O. Box 14520
New Bern, NC 28561

Copyright© 2015
Interior Text Design by Pamela S. Almore

ISBN: 978-0692561300

All rights reserved. Except for brief excerpts used in reviews, no portion of this work may be reproduced or published without expressed written permission from the author or the author's agent.

First Edition
Printed and bound in the United States of America

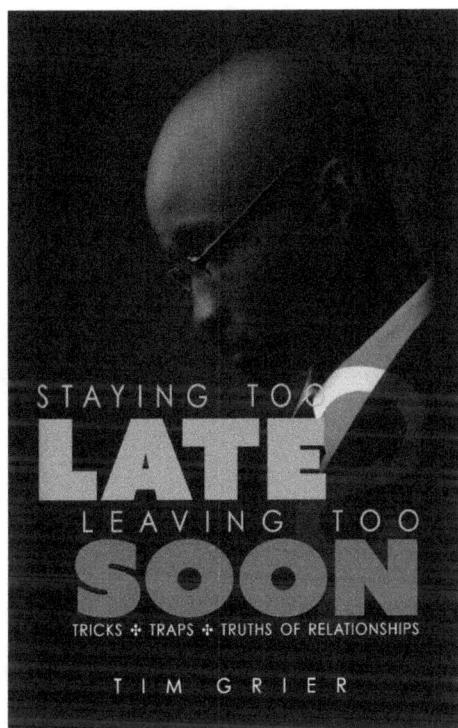

STAYING TOO
LATE
LEAVING TOO
SOON
TRICKS ✦ TRAPS ✦ TRUTHS OF RELATIONSHIPS

TIM GRIER

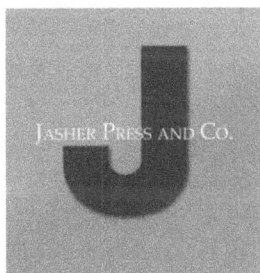

JASHER PRESS AND CO.

TABLE OF CONTENTS

INTRODUCTION: TRICKS- TRAPS- TRUTH 9
VITAL SIGNS 15
REMEMBER: 50
THE IMPATIENT & LONELY STAGE 63
DID I STAY TOO LATE LEAVE TOO SOON? 97
THE MODIFYING STAGE 119
ARE YOU READY STAGE? 151
ABOUT THE AUTHOR 217

To my Big mama- The late Sadie Allen and my Loving mother –The late Rachel Boyd. These two ladies were the epitome of true love. I sincerely thank them for all they instilled in me, and challenging me to become the man that I am today.

To my loving wife of 20 yrs. Angie. It is through blood, sweat, and tears, and victory we have survived it…to tell it. To all my kids, Jasmine, Crystal, Brittany, Brianna, Jonquez and all my little grandchildren 7 of them Wow!!!

Acknowledgement- To my Spiritual Father, Bishop Kevin L. Long the greatest Pastor, friend, counselor one could ask for. Thank you, for support, encouragement, and accountability. The great people of Temple Church International (TCI). To all my family and my friends…I SAY THANK YOU FOR BELIEVING IN ME.

TRICKS- TRAPS- TRUTH

THIS IS A MILLON DOLLAR QUESTION. DID I STAY
TOO LATE/ OR LEAVE TOO SOON?

From the (Griertionary) – **Relationship** – is where two
people share in a likeness, listening, and a learning
experience that they both can apply, appeal to, and
appreciate. Interdependence meets uniqueness, and
uniqueness respects individuality. There is an impact of
thought, the evolving of expression, passion, and the
sincerity of heart brings about a collective bond.
Relation Trap – It is when two persons have the
momentum of going nowhere fast.
Therefore, they find themselves ending up in something, or
somewhere, with someone they never intended. The effort
to release and be free has become futile. Now the
contention contradicts the desire, and creates the stigma,
which holds it bondage.

Hello My Friend,

I wanted to take this time to extend appreciation that is due unto you. The consideration you have given, taking the time to read this book honors me greatly! This is not another book about 12 steps on how to do this or that. This is not a book to show how great women are, or how sad men can be. This is not a book to dictate your choices. However, to consider if the one you have made, or are MAKING is correct. I will not try to control your anxieties (even though we might need it). I will not attempt to make you promises that you may not want, OR KEEP anyway.

Nevertheless, if you will allow me I would like to talk to you, and your mind.

Please take in consideration during this discussion, the challenges that will take place. I do believe we will come to one conclusion; either I am in a **Relationship or a Relation Trap**.

This journey starts with some profound statements and thought provoking questions.

1   Should I stay or go?
2   Is it over?
3   Why did I ever?
4   If I leave, will I ever do it again?
5   What would have happened if I had just waited?
6   Could this finally be the one?
7   When is it enough? DO THEY EVEN LOVE ME? Do I LOVE THEM?

Profound but true; these are all valid and often pondered. Most time, we are bombarded or absorbed by these types of questions. In their validity, but without caution we are introduced to the state of melancholy. Let me ask you a question. When is the right time to make the conscious/correct choices?

Is it before you enter? Once you get in? Is it when you are trying to exit out? Whatever your answer may be, a resolve is essential for your sanity. Every single answer is on the inside of you. Nevertheless, they are often hindered by your personal neglect.

Relationship or Relation Trap?

I have always said that relationships are either fun, or can be fatal. I also believe that they can possibly fall under three categories:

1. They are **immature**- you know impulsive, spontaneous- these types just happen without no clue of what is next. Anything will happen, but preparation is not on the agenda. They will have rash expectations, exaggerated negatives, and idealize positives. Be careful!

2. **Premature**- these are undeveloped- untrained- inexperienced- these have no business in operation. They are not ready to happen, and more than often negative consequences are a norm because of the "I need it, or got to have it" attitude. They have no clue of resolve. These are driven by mostly selfish gain. There will be signs of some type of manipulation found lurking. This one is never considerate of anyone's feelings.

Some examples:
- Your love is more like a burden, than a blessing
- Violence becomes a part
- You feel miserable most of the time
- There is always a pondering of when it will get better.

In your observation, you realized it want.

3. **Mature**- Are familiar with words like: established- honorable –respectful- time – attention - trust-faith-patience-kindness with the understanding these are just a few which causes growth and health in this

11

relationship. This one has positive energy, ready to combat negative enemies and emotions. It holds assurance, creativity, and has a great sense of value. The fact is: in this relationship, each individual is a **person not an object.**

One thing must happen: we can never blame anyone for the recognition of our own responsibility to know who they are. It is incumbent upon you and I to recognize the inevitable.

Now it is decision time!

Do I become proactive? Do I remain reactive, ultimately leaving me inactive?

What I know or do not know may cause or retain my unstableness. Can I help you? **Contemplation and ignorance often hangs out together.**

When it comes time to making some foundational choices, why do we tend to grasp selective amnesia?

So then Tim what is too long? What is too soon?

I believe that in some cases: 2 minutes can be too long, and in others, 2 years can be too soon. I need you to understand, timing is everything.

EITHER RUNNING IS A REALITY OR STAYING IS A LASTING SOLUTION.

Whatever the case; **there is Education that comes from the Experience**, which often appears in both. My friend, in every experience there is the exposure of education. Now the common question must be; what are we learning from it all?

Now answer this question:

Free or trapped???
The pressure of my intuition vs. The persuasion of their influence
This is literally the thoughts I had originally, battling their provoking and prevailing thoughts I wrestle with now. Yes I am talking to you. One minute you in it, the next you want out. One minute you are in love, the next hatred has taken over. The warfare between the initiation and the influence is a never-ending saga.

The question is still on the table: **Do I have a relationship, or am I battling another relation trap?**
We are forever trying to figure this out.
Do I hang on pretending?
Do I leave curious?
Do I enter or reenter apprehensively?
The decision-making cannot be delusional; it must be concrete. Things are never a requirement... they are always optional. **However, what we choose not to make a requirement, renders us our most struggle.**
LET'S TALK!
Why do we get out of something temporarily going bad, that could be eternally good?
For something, that is temporarily good, eternally going bad. Watch out!
Watch this! It has the momentum but no maturation.**NO MATURATION, NO DURATION.**
If not careful, you will be forced into their desires and delusions, without ever realizing your destiny. **It was never designed for you to be alone, but it was never designed for you to live in bondage**
That is why this book is so important.

1 To the single mother trying to raise a family, and looking for someone to join in

2   A single dad paralyzed by deception, emasculation and even manipulation
3   That pre-marital anxiety that is spontaneous without pre-caution
4   That divorce between contemplation and activation
5   That so called "perfect relationship" with no adherence to wisdom
6   That special one, but you still have too many uncertainties

This book is how we impatiently select without reflection, or continue without a clear perspective. The anxiety that comes with belonging, confines us to a mindset that does not release our freedom. So we chase fantasy and features, but not quite sure if they secure our future. When we fail to pursue knowledge, then it's our ignorance that consumes us. Educating ourselves is imperative. True relationships are God given, and not feeling driven. The power and the presence of unconditional terms, and unwavering faith that ties two people together with an uncommon love will validate the relationship.

This one is all-inclusive, but none exclusive. When we finish our discussion, there will be one conclusion and one only.

We are heading in one!
We need to come out of one!
We cannot believe the power that exist from this one we have!

An old Proverb says, (paraphrased) that the prudent man looks and perceives, and makes the adjustment. However, the fool looks, ignores and then is destroyed by his refusal. I see the problem, I ignore the problem, now the problem overtakes me. If at all necessary; let's make all the necessary adjustments.

CHAPTER 1

VITAL SIGNS

When we look at vital signs, we understand that we have to evaluate the function.

Therefore, my friend these are important: **pressure, temperature, pulse, body& breath** all need undivided attention for optimal performance, welfare, and survival of the relationship.

Can I ask you a few questions?

1. HOW MUCH TENSION IS THERE? - How much is being created? PRESSURE
2. DO YOU KNOW THE PULSE (HEART BEAT) OF THE OTHER PERSON?-PULSE
3. IS THIS RELATIONSHIP HOT- COLD- JUST LUKE WARM? – TEMPERATURE
4. Does IT HAVE LIFE? CAN IT BE RESUSCITATED? OR IS IT DOA-DEAD ON ARRIVAL?- **BREATH**

You truly do not have to answer me, but you just might want to ask and answer yourself. It would behoove you to take all these things in consideration. This is before going in, or re-entering, or even coming out. Did you know normally we take 12to 20 breaths per minute. However, because we become so absorbed by our indecisiveness, our anxiety increases, while our optimal breathing decreases. Now the chances, that would sustain a positive relationship stands at a minimum zero chances.

The word of God declares; that we should have life, and have it more abundantly.

Here is the problem. We unconsciously design enemies, which steal, kill, and destroy our maximum output. Thereby, leaving input at best stagnant, and even in most cases nonexistent. Who are the enemies? They are people, who we allow to tamper with our lives, without our wellbeing as a priority. They do not carry the necessary credentials, but are afforded the opportunity to practice. These persons use the tool of deception (we will talk about in this selective phase) to lure you in to their arena. Here is the dilemma. **THE POWER AND THE POSITION YOU PUT THEM IN, OFTEN IS THE POWER AND THE POSITON THEY USE AGAINST YOU.**

All of this is a direct hit; because we do not check the signs. I found out; people love practicing on those who will not hold them accountable, and who recognizes that we are lethargic about checking for the necessary signs.

My friend, not checking your own signs or their credentials allows the opportunity for mal practice.

Mal Practice-The negligence or misconduct or mistreatment resulting in injury or damage

Did you catch that!

They fail to meet the standard care or conduct CONCERNING YOU. However, you fail to conduct a standard test concerning them. It's not that they don't know what to do, but with you they just practice it incorrectly. This is common in relation traps. When you keep giving them permission to repeat these unethical cycles. They will always fail to meet the standard care, because you allow it.

16

YOU DO NOT NEED EXPERIMENTING ON! BUT YOU ALLOW IT.

There has to be a <u>standard</u>. Why do we give people permission to corrupt our minds, and tamper with our hearts, knowing they do not have the wherewithal to CARE FOR us? You have to be loved right and properly cared for. STOP RIGHT HERE! SAY IT! **I MUST BE PROPERLY CARED FOR!** Do not grow timid about feelings right now. I DARE YOU TO DECLARE IT. I just made my announcement... now make yours.

When should I make it? Let's make it before you go in – after you get in- and even if you have to come out. What is the announcement? I am so glad you ask!

FRAGILE... HANDLE ME WITH CARE!
You have to be loved right! DON'T DARE Stop until they get it/ and you understand it, and BOTH appreciate it.
NOT ANOTHER ONE...practice to you perfect it.

By no means do I claim to be the voice on relationships. However, I have been around, seen, experience and even counseled enough, to know there is some relational mal-practicing going on. Yes, I am talking you! The damage has been done. I am one just bold enough to expose it. It will not harm you – hurt you- or hinder you any longer. Please realize **you are free... now be free indeed.** Either you are going to get your joy back or you going to put a stop to those which try to steal it. **If there are no credentials, there should not be the relinquishment of the essentials.** You cannot allow just anyone the opportunity. <u>What seems to be an opportunity</u> could very well be a <u>disguised opposition.</u>

The question is still on the floor. **Am I in a relationship or a relation trap?**

17

Whatever changes, enhancements, or decisions need to be made, let us begin to make them **NOW!** You have to excuse me; but in my concern I will apply a little pressure.

Right here: write down the person or persons you have allowed to come in, and cause injury. Name-how long it has persist- the place- every detail. Its freedom time!!!!!

Before we move further: forgive yourself!!!!

When I decided to write, I asked God to reveal his mysteries for this book. I did not want to seem like the guru, the professor, or the master voice. I wanted people to realize the destiny in having it or the dangers of doing it, doing it again without knowledge or doing it without the right mindset.

This is what I figured out:

1. People do not know how to handle **YOU WITH CARE!**
2. **YOU** don't make it mandatory- or
3. **Because it goes undetected when it is available, it is often rejected, and unappreciated**

Very few people fall in love with (you) the person. They fall in love with your attributes (what you can do -not who you are). When this is the case, it can become conditional driven. Let me ask you something. Whatever happened to real relationships?

They use to be passionate and compassionate. Now, they are substituted by possessiveness/ and selfishness. The relinquishment of its excitement, has been halted by the penalty of pain. It seems this day and time; that relationships are too conditional driven. More than often, the attribute outweighs and even outlast the authenticity.

So see the dominance that comes with these so-called "attributes" repeatedly extends the absenteeism of authentic love. There is no harm intended. It maybe your sex, political power, your religious posture or your money and

material acquirements but very rare dependable and down-to-earth love. **Now you may be real and ready, but your love MAY not always be their reality.**
Okay Tim, I hear that. Nevertheless, something always draws you. You are right.
But what happens when that which has drawn you, doesn't desire or carry the capacity to retain you or the relationship.
On the other hand, what they presented or you presented originally, no longer carries the strength nor the energy for the duration, needed for a healthy/ productive relationship.

This may need to be Q&A TIME for u. Whatever you do, please do not disregard these moments. You cannot guess, you must know. RELATIONSHIP OR RELATION TRAP???
DELIMMA:
1. **The money start depleting**
2. **The sex start derailing**
3. **The power start dimming**
4. **The fun starts decaying**
5. **The love starts declining**

We get in trouble, because we often make these things the basis of our relationships. However, in heart they quickly, but assuredly become our tumbling. Bishop Kevin LONG Says: *"Esthetics doesn't mean Ethics."*
Yes, I am talking to you! What you thought as an attribute; has now changed its mind and its passion. <u>I told you; if you do not make it mandatory, they want consider that they have to. I</u> know you had, or yet have good intentions. I have a little secret for you. **Your original <u>intentions</u> are not always productive enough to keep their undivided attention.**
My friend, what we fail to look for or even demand initially; may expeditiously drive us to the culmination of the relationship. Conditional people are not accustomed to

or with unconditional love. That is why the "**selective phase**" is vital. People base love and relations off emotional stimulation. **Presentation more than often becomes problematic**. Can you explain? Yes, I will.

The very thing you or the person depended on for the relationship's duration expires pre-maturely. Now you are left dumfounded, for not understanding or demanding the essentials necessary for the production of a true relationship.

Let me ask you a few questions.

- What are your priorities? What is theirs?
- What is your perspective?
- What type of people have you been entertaining and/or accepting?

As we enter into this selective phase, notice that people may come and go for the wrong reasons. Once again, without being redundant, people do not consider your desires over their wishes. These type of questions may never be viewed as important. Just because you don't consider that; your wellbeing may always be devalued.

Hate to hit you with this bombshell; you may not be a priority you may be just a conditional craving (just for the time being). Sorry!

1   We have been together a long time. Sorry!
2   We are just getting serious. Sorry!
3   I just went and bought the ring. Sorry!
4   We just had a child together. Sorry!
5   That was the best sex anyone could ever have! Sorry!
6   We have been praying together. Do not mean any harm. Sorry!
7   I said I do. Guess what! Sorry! Even at the altar, it still might be sorry

Sometimes in the worst case scenarios the results are disappointing.

You must make proper selections in the right frame of mind, not just by incentive.

If not you will never be able to differentiate between the two.

When you are my Priority – you are my main concern- you take precedence- you are my preference- you do not have to ask to be these things… you just are.

When you are my Craving – you are my desired consumption for the time- you will fill the need for now- I desire you for now- **but when I change my mind, I'll change you.** You are the void **filler or just an option. When I finish with you as my option, then you become obsolete.**

Just know that **a circumstance does not always create the passion. The emphasis they put on their need, may expel your want, if silence becomes your option.**

1. You want to be loved- they just need sex/ and a bank.
2. You want a family- they just need you for as parental participation.
3. You want a relation- they just need someone to help rebound their feelings, or numb their pain. Circumstances does not create the passion, or the relationship. Most of our penalties received, are from unethical presentations.

Hey, I got an announcement! THE LONGER YOU BE QUIET, THE LONGER THEY NEED YOU TO BE!

It's in our insufficiency that ignorance supplies the most delusions. One again the questions has to be:

1. What principles am I making my decisions by?
2 what drives my selections?
3 where does these emotions come from?
4- Is your selections formed from unconscious motives and thoughts?

21

It does not take a rocket scientist to discover that something is wrong. **It is not with people you choose; but the choices that limit you to only keep choosing those kind. Now it is decision time…**
I found out; that a damage past- dismal views- or a desperate mind are major flaws in selecting. Explain please….
When we fail to rule in our attitudes and articulations, we limit our control. My friend, your attitude and your actions play such a major role in selecting, retaining and even exiting. **There must be a devotion and a discipline. The devotion can be violated by the temptation.** Hey, it will always show up in your selections.

Damage Past: This hurt comes from a previous that often brings a fear of loneliness. If not careful, you will select the same old person in a different body. See when we refuse to take our time, because we didn't take time to heal, we get in a hurry. And my friend, **hurry don't help you heal. However, hurry hastens your havoc.** (Next chapter) So even though we find a new person, it's a familiar spirit. That spirit knows your spirit, that's why it continues to introduce to you, what it knows you already like. What do you mean? The very thing that you say you hate, you find yourself loving. (Oxymoronic)

Thereby, **the struggle to get away from it, meets the resistance to stay around it.** So you make them a priority, while you are becoming their consumption. Now the open wounds of yesterday cannot, and will not be healed. Why? Because the damage, which initiates the hurry keeps the wound open, and accessible to infection. Then we extend it to someone who can't help heal it, but will help hurt it. The extension of our pain become co-dependent on our reminders. **The evidence of those things remaining, is because the presence of those things that reminds us. Warning!!!!! The danger of starting a new one, MAY be affected by the lingering residue of the old one. Be**

Careful right here! It's the residue that rids the relationship of success. <u>**ANY RELATIONSHIP trying to take off or restart will be either rigid or become reckless if there's no resolve from the residue.**</u> Some people leave, stay, or re-enter because of "personal infectious cravings'. In my own experience (we will talk later) found out that **personal satisfaction, may allude us to personal dysfunction**. Notice when it is not about you, or when it is too much about them (vice versa), the ability to accommodate each other's need can become a strain. The #1 enemy to any and every type of relationship is **Selfishness**.

Selfish people do not share…even in relationships

<u>So you are waiting on them to release love, when they have only been self –trained to receive for themselves not relinquish to you.</u> **THEY DO NOT KNOW HOW TO RELEASE; SO BE CAREFUL HOW YOU RELINQUISH.**

Relationships that are pursuing marriage, reuniting, not looking to separate or starting up this is very important. **One of the biggest problems in selecting; is often we forget that we count**. We become so co-dependent on their feelings, then our selection can take a total blank. <u>Once the recognition of stupidity is in play, then their selfishness, and your ignorance, becomes the pattern</u>, and the problem.

My friend, I have learned one thing: **either you are intimidated by their influence, or they are influenced by your ignorance.**

Dismal view: Most times people will not promote your stableness, or your soundness, because it takes away from their selfishness. **When you fail to see, you will eventually see where you have failed.** We too often fabricate these fantasies

Truth be known, you know who you want, how you want them to look, when, where, what and even why. That is not the problem. The problem occurs when your desires and what GOD designs for you; becomes non-compliant by them. When this occurs, you are tampering on dangerous grounds. You may be or they may be inviting the act of compulsivity. What do you mean?

<u>Compulsions are habitual behaviors or mental acts an individual is driven to perform in order to reduce stress and anxiety.</u>

Could this be some of the problems in our selection phase? The fact that what we are dealing with may be a pre-conceived notion as a reducer for our stress, or curving our anxieties. That is why their cravings or yours take over any potential. I don't mean any harm. So we start using sex, substances, and other substitutions to cover up our numbness or even worse make us feel good about our desperate, and deluded decisions.

Now let us look: this could be the reason why we are in and out of so many relationships. We are impulsive (thoughtless), until it becomes compulsive. One minute we are so hasty (cannot wait) the next, we have become habitual (same old stuff different person). We don't mean to be like this; however, we can't stop. **It is the unintentional that become habitual.** These habit-forming selections, produce by our negative circumstances and anxieties, then introduces us to our next **relation trap.** Then we look for people to accept our mistakes; but they are not mistakes, they are now habits camouflaged. This dismal view is mostly evident in our dysfunctional behavior, which brings with it, our irresponsibility and vulnerability. When your vulnerability is recognized, you will not be appreciated for your true value. **How valuable you are to yourself, has to override, how vulnerable they believe you are to them.** The physician Freud believes: there are unconscious forces in the personality that cause our problem. The idea is grasped in the fact, the visible disturbances in people's behavior, and the emotions reflect invisible disorder in their personality. This is why

24

selection is vital. You might be excited about curtain #1 but what is behind it, may need to be the real question. **They may have external features, but can't secure a productive future!**

My friend, we fail because there's not an adequate appreciation of who we are, and adequate understanding of who they may be. So you see; Freud is right in his assessments. Yes I do concur. I also say: that if there is no order in your relationships, chaos is an inevitable. See so many times after we have been damage, instead of healing, we go on a hunt to bring people into our chaotic world, and expect/ demand the relationship to be functional and normal. Can I help?

Watch this! **Some of our selections are routine; but so is our pain, and so is our outcome.**

See my friend, the survival rate of you coming out of a negative one or going in a positive is almost zero to none. See when we limit our investigation; we lack the fullness, and the capacity that this relationship could bring. **<u>It is after we have been damage; that we tend to lose appreciation for who we have been created to be.</u>** Can I help? Most times people didn't become that way, they already were. Here is the problem. They didn't have to reveal it you. Why you may ask? It was in your blindness; that gave them the permission to keep it disguised. The only thing they did at this point, was intensify their character that was there from the beginning. **Remember: sometimes 2 minutes can be too long. Here is the sadness. We take the 2 minute drill and turn it into 20 years only to declare "frustrated and unhappy." It is not now this unhappiness has occurred... it is you have just chose to be true to what has always been there.**

Why you may ask? The anxiety of being alone (we talk about in the impatient &lonely stage phase) or the anxiety that causes the fear of starting another one. **The presence of this pain could be the result of a pressured and panic**

pick. Am I telling the truth yet? You did not stop until you had to have **this one**. Now it is this one, or was that one that seems to reinforce uninvited pain. **Sometimes they do not have to be there to do the damage; it is what they said or done that has an everlasting effect.**

Dr Larry Crabb says: *"We fail because of confused and shallow understanding of people and their problems."*

My friend, it is mighty funny how we pick our pain and help our hurt. *There is a way that seems right, but in the end the road leads to destruction.* ***(Proverbs 14:12)***

Can I ask you a question? Did we forget to love ourselves; then create a dependency on someone, or something else for sustaining?

At what point did we miss detachment time. **I do <u>understand there is not always running at the first sign; but I also understand that you sure as hell do not have to hang around to see the last sign.</u>** I know they were all that and a bag of chips. **If even though they were all that to you; you may have not been none of that to them. The** selection phase and the vital signs are important. Here is the problem. Whether it's accurate assessment, or assumption; we tend to celebrate surface thoughts and feelings. WATCH OUT!!!! In your celebration, we fail to realize that it may be a deeper issue, that's creating a deeper problem. **Remember: what we choose to ignore, we choose to ignite.**

I must challenge you here to be very careful in your approach; it may have a dismal effect on your reception. **It is in our ability to quickly receive, that we become quickly deceived. The sign of a dismal view is often evident, by our dysfunctional, and delusional picks. (It's called panic picks) Be careful!**

My friend, people are personal- rational- volitional- and emotional. **<u>This is why it is important that we do our homework before we have to do the hard work.</u>** The tension that comes with having the perfect person, and the

26

flawless relationship; often hastens and intensifies our dysfunctions and desperations. The lack of evaluation of ourselves, most times is a prelude to the disaster that renders the relationship ineffective, and non-productive. The history of our failures, should have educated us before the next experience, but very rare is it afforded the opportunity. Why you may ask? So many times; it is our stubbornness that presents our resistance from the education and the reality.

Warning!!!!! You may be prioritizing senselessness and desensitizing stability.

Relationships are built off truth, and not fabrication. If you cannot present or allow them to present the actual, then the relationship starts as a lie. This should be a part of the selection phase. Remember it's not just what you want, it is also who you are. Please let's be true to thy self. **You either have recuperated and are ready; or in a process of getting it together and you are not. Often times in the selection phase, dependency brings the dilemma. When things are conditionally driven, the things you essentially need, tends to become isolated by the things you initially wanted. Now who you really are, takes a back seat to who you are pretending to be.**

 Let's take a min and write down your essential needs list- Now ask yourself when have I followed it, while requiring others to so?

Its right here where your vulnerability can/ and will be detected. Once this happens your value depreciates. **People who see that you don't see, value the fact that they can keep you blind.** Remember: we attract who we are. This is why the selection phase is important, and precaution is essential. If there is no precaution, I can assure you; there will always have to be a reaction. Please don't miss this! **We ARE PENALIZE BY WHAT WE DO NOT PRIORITIZE.**

Stop- hold up- wait a minute!!!!!!

Please be careful! Desperation is starting to lurk and it is looking for you. If by chance it finds you... your anxiety will help it unconsciously make the wrong choices. I don't mean any harm. We often make these selections, based off these things:

1   Compulsion- feeling forced
2   Complexity – harder my life, the eager my choices (panic picking)

We are overflowing with these anxieties to tolerate another relation trap. Watch This! **While we fail in the area of compatibility, we often excel in the arena of complex.** You always worrying about the very thing that keeps you in a frenzy.

Most relationships are damage from the beginning because of:

- Improper perspectives
- Insignificant selections-Insensitive people

The right person with you at the wrong time, or the wrong person with you at the perceived right time will not work. This is why uncertainty will keep any relationship from being intact. Don't mean any harm. What we tend to accept, we like to keep, and will not exchange it, even if it means our demise. The word of God says this: be anxious for nothing, but in everything with prayer and supplication, make your request known unto God. (Philippians 4:6)

Let me ask you a question. When was the last time you prayed? I mean for real, before you went in, while you were in it, or made a decision to come out of it. My friend, I will not bombard you with a bunch of scriptures. Nevertheless, I feel obligated to tell you **pray before you play.** If you do not adhere to this advice; the more you feel the need to play, the more the need will make you bow, and pray. As a matter of fact, let us pause briefly.

Whisper this prayer:

Dear lord, help me with my decision-making. Amen

Had you scared thought we were going to pray for the rest of the book. No, I have much more to say. We are going to have some fun, after we get free in our minds.

My friend, it is sad to know that which is causing your pain, in most cases, it is inspired by your support. Remember: Self affliction (disorder) is often caused by on our selections. **We are effected bywhat we keep doing to ourselves.**

Please try to understand in the selection phase, **impostor presentations are hazardous.**

Tim what is that? It is the act of practicing deception on someone else, using an assumed character to bring solidarity and validity to the relationship. Okay! You are playing games from the beginning. The problem is that this is not you; it is just your momentary character presentation. Here is what makes it hazardous: When you try to retire that role, the one who you selected to accompany you in it, handles you base on that role only. **Warning!!!!!!!!**

They are only prepared to handle you based on that role you presented; not what you intended.

What do you mean?

1. If you act disreputable(even though you are not) your treatment will disrespectful
2. If you act as you are a goffer (one who falls for anything, or goes for anything) your treatment will be as such
3. If you act desperate (even though you are not) you know the treatment.

I do not mean any harm. **They will never see you pass your definition of yourself.**

Don't be crazy! **These are confused people themselves, they have just mastered how to keep theirs hidden, because yours stay more accessible.**

29

The thing that follows us: is we tend to have some of the same behaviors, beliefs and even baggage that keep representing itself, as we anticipate something different. Problem is we keep making the same choices. My friend, too often: **we look for the perfect person, while in return we hide our dysfunctions.** Not realizing it is our dysfunctions that strengthen them, and weakens us. I found out: that people are personal, and they long deeply- think strongly, who to choose and how to feel about their choices. **Problem-** we often fabricate these fantasies and disregard realities. In doing this: we have perfected picking our pain and helping our hurt.

It is sad to know, and becomes even worse when it's you that aids in your own affliction. More than often self-inflictions are directed by self-afflictions. **Not only do I cause the pain, but I force the pain**. What is unfortunate that I allow myself, more forceful panic picks. My friend, make sure discernment is used. If no discernment; it could increase the disorder and spell out your disaster. Too many times we pre-celebrate our surface thoughts, only to be frustrated over again, later by deeper details that we originally ignored. Remember: what you choose to ignore; you select to ignite. I know the urge was so penetrating. Tim, you just don't know. Oh believe me, I do. Here is the problem. You had a chance to select (the right one, in the right time) but took on the challenge, anticipating the change, not knowing you never stood a chance.

That is why you cannot play, and present yourself as an impostor. You must know who you are, and whose you are. If not careful, you will confuse <u>your time of fragments</u> (when you are trying to find all the pieces) as a time trying to present yourself as whole. Watch this! Only to be torn in pieces again. **<u>It is not just what you selected, it is what you have accepted</u>. While you were accepting, you never realized you were becoming an exception.** Be careful! You may start feeling inferior, while making them feel superior. Sad as it may be, the vulnerability that comes with inferiority could be what keeps drawing these relation traps. Why? Vulnerability can be viewed as a sign of weakness. Unlike you, this how people make a lot of their selections, in their vulnerable times. It's when we are not quite coherent, so we irrationally choose. It's in our unawareness that we lose the possibility of being sure, only settling for uncertainty. I don't mean any harm… **But, it is in our weakest moments; that we take on our weakest members.**

Be careful! **Most relationships that don't last, are a result of pre-selection in times of weakness. As long as we don't understand this; we will become submissive to a definition that only contradicts a godly design.** This in return starts, and creates an everlasting bondage of more bad choices. Selfish people who see this; are captivated by it, this means they will not appreciate the value that you possess. Your weakness has overtaken them, and destabilized you.

You think you are ready. You thought you were ready. You are confident it is ready. Well, it starts in the selection phase. You cannot limit your expectations, on even concur that they have the capacity and the capability to comprehend you. Why is that?

They may know your vulnerability, without accepting your value.

Remember: they have no clue of who you are. <u>**Because what you presented, is not what God had preserved.**</u>

Sometimes if we are not cautious in our quest to start one- restart one- or even keep one, we will **forsake our future for fantasy.**

My friend, sometimes our vision is obscured by our condition or our traditions. They both carry enough weight by themselves to keep us incomprehensible to proper selecting. Many times our selections are <u>rebounds filled</u>

<u>with moments of anxiety</u>, that the clearance and the clarity for love seems farfetched.

Warning!!!!

Right here! We begin to limit ourselves... **We go through the experience, then refuse the lesson.** It is the lesson that wants to keep us from repeating. But since we refuse to learn, we perpetuate the cycles. **Warning!!!!!!!!!! If not careful you will become addicted to abusing yourself. Remember: most of our afflictions are self-inflicted.**

Do not abandon yourself; by becoming addicted to them. The consideration you give them, may not be capacity that they carry for you. Know this! YOU MAY SELECT THEM, THEY MAY OBLIGUE YOU- IT DOES NOT MEAN THEY HAVE SELECTED YOU. **REMEMBER: FANTASY DOES NOT MEAN FUTURE!!!! Do not confuse their satisfaction, for the relationship duration. Sorry!**

We go on these pursuits to find perfection, only to find the penalties of our pick. His name is PAIN. Once the cycle is in repeat mode; the destructive patterns become more evident, and present a no other choice mentality. My friend, this misguided notion opens you up to victimization. Sorry to inform you; but this is the reasoning behind why we settle. We start out, settle for these pre-conditional relations that only render us empty all over again. **Now if not careful we celebrate our choices, while tolerating our distractions at the same time. Relationship or another relation trap?**

ANSWER THIS!

Why do we continue to try to make these **no** persons be our **yes people**? What do you mean? You know **yes people: the ones who we fanaticize, and romanticize about, who we just got to have no matter what. Regardless of what they do, how the act, they are the one.**

Here is the problem! These people will give you every sign they are not the one. However, because of willful blindness, you chose not to adhere. They keep showing you, I am not the one. I told you previously, that stupidity is not a requirement. When you refuse to refuse, then you penalize yourself, and paralyze any other options.

These imaginary yes people will always warn you, before they show you. However, since you are convinced, it is almost effortless to contend with your conviction.

Big mama use to say, **"Can't tell you nothing with your hard head".** Watch this! At some point, you will start receiving what you did not fight, figure out or fix in the beginning. My friend, you have become so consumed, with the idea of having a relationship, you have now entered into a **relation trap.**

Please understand, that selfish people only benefit from your ignorance, but repelled by your intelligence. The less deposits you refuse to make, the more withdrawals they will. Remember: how vulnerable you are to them, only comes from you not realizing how valuable you should be to yourself.

This will always determine the difference between a relationship and the relation trap. My friend, the relationship is and will always be ruined by insensitivity. This insensitivity is manifested in insecurity, also instability. **The power of loving yourself; is not allowing others to treat you lesser. Challenge - QUIT CREATING THESE TERMS OF ENDEARMENT, WHICH YOU ARE NOT WILLING TO FOLLOW. Terms requested, but never followed is only hypocrisy.** What do you mean? List of Do's that you don't. You know:

- Affection needed
- Admiration needed

- Honesty/ integrity wanted

But for some reason you never apply to yourself; what you require of others. You must first hold yourself responsible, and accountable for treatment, before extending the requirement. **Know this: people never will respond by appreciation, what you devalue**. Let me ask you something. Why should they carry the burden of making sure you are happy, when you don't put a demand on it? **Be careful!!! You must not expect the endurance from them; when there is no self- assurance from you.**

I was looking through a site, and the statement was made "learn how to choose you over anyone who would make you feel different about yourself." I believe we spend too much time chasing connections that would cause you, not to be a better you. **Remember: why you are focused on them; don't forget about yourself. No accountability, sometimes is interpret as no responsibility.**

Let me ask you a question. Why do we keep giving into situations that present relationship standards, but only produce relation trap status. Look at the trail mix:

- It leaves you angry/ bitter
- Condescending
- Suspicious
- Manipulating
- Confused
- Irritated

BUT NEVER SATISFIED…

Once again, when it does not carry reliable affection, your selection will begin to turn IT another direction. I don't mean any harm. BUT you cannot get upset for the lack of their adjustment. You must hold yourself accountable for the constant lustful anxiety that stems from you, and the consistency of negative consequences you continue to receive. Now pretending becomes common way of living the lie. Watch out!!!! **YOUR PRETENDING, WILL**

LINK YOU TO WISHFUL THINKING. Yes people only go with the game if it is a benefit to them. **Please understand what you are presenting by pretension, may not be an absolute.** When we are not cautious in our selection phase, the collapsing novelty will expedite the relationship to a close. Sometimes there will be a warning, and sometimes it will be spontaneous. It saddens me, when I talk to people, who know that their selection was a <u>no</u> from the beginning. **May I call you to the carpet? LET'S TELL THE TRUTH. You knew they were an exit, when you entered.**
So why do we look for life in what we know has already expired???

This is a sad moment:
1. **We want people to kill what we created**
2. **Heal our chosen hurts**
3. **Punish our picks**
4. **Bring solidarity to our stupidity**
5. **And even negotiate with our negligence**

The sign said exit, you invented an entrance, now hopelessness has shown it face again.
Well Tim, people can change. I did not say that. <u>But I will say, some don't change their character, they just work hard at pulling you out of yours.</u> See once all the effort and the vigor go into changing them, the less time they will use to convince you otherwise. I do not mean any harm. They have one conclusion; there is no need for a disguise. Your desperation has ushered in your blindness. Be careful! Your indulgence could very well be at its peak level. Your greed for need takes over. **Now your selection is without pre-caution, and YOUR acceptance is without discernment. Is it a relationship or a relation trap?**
Be careful! Sometimes decision making, goes without careful consideration. If you are only guided by emotions

and feelings without sufficient data, you could be misled into another relation trap. See one of the main problems: **is not how I have been treated by others, but how I have treated myself.** It often amazes me how we dress confusion up... and then call her "stable". Our acceptance does not modify, it only intensifies in increments. This means: that the turmoil of our choices does not all of sudden just appear. In a relation trap the individual will not all at once reveal true their character. He /she has to allow the drainage of the characteristic to exhaust all. Remember: it is not about who you are, but what you can produce for the endurance. Now the invitation for you to believe, accept, and even condone their behavior, brings credence to their attack. Here is the problem. You have not recognized your part in it all. What is my part? Your part is stupidity- and their part will always be selfishness. Once again we dress it up and call it a stable relationship; but in retrospect it is a **relation trap.**

I AM REALLY TRYING TO HELP!

My friend, just know when your blinders are on, when you decline to see, why should they be convince otherwise. People know that your desperation will not detect, neither discern their deliberate state of mind. I found out (Mike Murdock) "what are willing to put up with, we will not change it."

The question is: why should I hide who I am, if you are already lost in who you should be. My # 1 job if you are confused is to keep you confused. Please don't expect more- if you continuously show me less. I showed you, I was not the one; but since you insist, I will assist, in what you would not resist, and it will persist.

The reality of who they were was initially there; but your unforeseen anxiety, complimented their disguise. Tim you are right! I entered an exit.

Remember: **2 minutes can be too long.** Exposure often comes not for your observation, but also warning you of what not to accept. Without discernment, and discipline your desire could be nothing more than a delusion and possible part of your destruction. **Now we are infected by what we selected.**

I have a little secret. People are trip!!!
They will play on your weakness, because this is how the gain their strength. They depend on what you don't see, to see more of what they want. While you are weakening from desperation, they are gaining or regaining off of your delusion.
Are you free? I DON'T THINK SO!

I have poem: **DELUSION will always bring confusion; confusion will bring an intrusion. The intrusion will direct you to a conclusion; and the conclusion will always look back at the start of the delusion. Don't fool yourself! PEOPLE** only gain access through insignificance. **Remember: if you remain quiet, then they need you to stay that way.**

The most powerful weapon you have against this; is to wake up to yourself, and gain awareness to their game.

These type of people, or selections, destroys marriages, devastate friendships or any potential relationships. They may not verbally be saying it, but continuously display to you, your wrong choice.

This is based off your weakness to stay, and increases their deception that want allow them to leave. They have this insatiable appetite for "stupidity". I know you are not calling me stupid. Of course not, I would not do that. However, the <u>thought</u> of you have staying, confuse, bound and unhappy; is quite irresponsible.

Remember: The more you remain weak; it is a reminder how strong they have perceived themselves to be.

They tricked you pass the 2minute mark.
?????? WHAT TIME DO YOU OPEN????

Until you open your eyes- your ears- to your destiny; your dysfunction will keep them closed.

YOU MIGHT NEED TO MAKE ANOTHER ANNOUNCEMENT RIGHT HERE!!!!
CLOSED FOR REMODELING!
UNDER CONSTRUCTION!
NO DIVING- RESTRICTED AREA!
OR
SORRY FOR THE INCONVIENCE CLOSED UNTIL FURTHER NOTICE!!!
DON'T BE ASHAME ABOUT SHUTTING DOWN FOR A SEASON.... IT'S PART OF YOUR COMEBACK!!!!
Warning! If you move to soon reopen too fast; it could set you back, instead of a comeback.

We have to stop! **We must stop volunteering our ignorance.** In this selection phase, there must be the sign of intelligence, not instability. I told you earlier. We forget to love ourselves, this negligence causes us to create a dependency on someone else. Then we expect them to do it for us. The mandate to love yourself is hindered by our maximized co-dependency. I don't mean any harm. The conclusion that they were non-compliant, and non – productive should settle one's suspicion, but more than often, it does not. Here is the dilemma. Now we unconsciously or even consciously commit to self-inflicted misery.

Now this is how you start gaining your strength back. You must admit it.

1. **Okay you hurt me**
2. **Okay I allowed it**
3. **Okay I was real stupid - I committed to lust and called it love**
4. **Okay you took it and ran**
5. **Okay I was pretty depressed- but stayed in anyway**

6. Okay I did not think I was going to make it- and knew you wasn't going to help

See once you can admit to your hurt, you have just committed to your help.

Be careful not to revive contentions and bondages in this quest of committing to yourself for a period. It is not that you are giving any credit to them; you are just regaining access to your sanity.

Please don't settle for just being a filling or just a feeling. You my friend, must be a fact to yourself and to them.

Remember: We pick our pain.

Sorry! The purpose that was intended by you, is not the always passion extended by them.

<u>So In your endeavors to become faithful to the things you do need; you find yourself confused with the things you don't.</u> Tim you have no idea. The more I try to get away from it, the more I like being around it. I believe I am in a relation trap.

You got to be more careful!

If not you will:

1. **Sanction your sinking**
2. **Promote your punishment**
3. **Uncover your uncontrollables**
4. **Amplify your addictions**

This selection is vital; because what you are willing to adopt, just know you are going to have to adapt. <u>Every selection is not bad, but the stigma of the ones that have been, more than often alters corrective judgment.</u>

Remember: once the recognition of your co-dependence on them is in place, you may be in trouble- the vast amounts of our selections based themselves off of your co-dependence.

Watch this! **When you are delusional, you cannot afford to take on more delusions, by accepting someone who is clueless to you and the necessary things for you.**

Why you may ask? I believe, we display a need to have someone fill our gap, and In the process of time, we lose the effort to love ourselves. Therefore, you partake in a selection, which is delusional not valid. Let me ask you a question.

Do you really love yourself? Well if you do, why does this disengagement keep presenting itself through improper selections?

Loving yourself is learning the art of not gravitating towards those who cannot reciprocate it in the confinements of the relationship.

Here is the trap:

1. **You have become irresponsible of self, and feel responsible for others**
2. **You anticipate their need for you**
3. **You feel you must distribute pleasure**
4. **You have created insecurity**
5. **You over commit for the access of love**
6. **You don't know how to detach**

I have created a poem just for you.

This is bad!

This is sad!

And before you know it, once again you have been had.

Watch this! You have become so obsessed with their affirmation; that your affection has intensified, through the attachment in which we refuse to depart.

So your mistake is not that you chose them; it is you have forgotten you.

Please be careful! Selection- Selection- Selection- Vital-Vital-Vital

Remember: they do not look for value- when they have found your vulnerability

My friend, this co-dependency introduces vulnerability, and the vulnerability introduces low self-value and apparent low self-esteem. So they become the recipient of the "best supporting actor" in the **no value** series.

Then we begin to create a list of characters:

1. Self- blame
2. Denial
3. Deprivation
4. Tough decision making
5. Negative beliefs

Be careful here! The conflict has aroused from a non-commitment to yourself. Explain….. When you are not true to yourself, then the toleration of them, becomes a normal way of life.

All this has become our normal way of thinking. Improper selections, has such an everlasting impact. I once believed the sensory of the unpleasant pain was the hilt. I have come to find out; it is the everlasting imprint of what you believe, and who you select.

Here is the issue: what you previously chose, now becomes the outlet of all your future choices. Remember we said: it is an everlasting imprint.

You keep choosing the same person, just in a different body. The question is still on the floor. **Is it a relationship or a relation-trap? Did I stay too late? Or have I left too soon.**

Hey, Tim I am losing it!!!!

1. **I am not checking vital signs**
2. **I am allowing people access to my mind and heart, who don't possess the credentials**
3. **I create fictional characters who I allow to exist, who really don't**
4. **I keep picking my pain- helping my hurt**
5. **I keep devaluing myself, and intensifying my vulnerability**
6. **I keep making arrangements with adversity**

41

OK stop and think! Ask yourself the original question.

Am I going in?

Am I staying in?

Do I really need to come out?

Are they capable of committing, and do you really want to commit to them?

Dr .Jefferey Gardere says: (I paraphrase) your persistent fantasies begin to override their persistent fear.

Granddaddy says: "study long, you study wrong". **The more time you spend on what if; should be spent on it can't be.** I believe the penalty of our reality, is the given production to our unproductive images. In every relation trap, this is an inevitable. If not careful, we will resurrect these images and succumb to another cycle that produces another lifeless relationship.

My friend, it is in the moment of deliberation, that intrigue sets in.

Elder, what do you mean?

At the point, you put some thought in to it, the deception begins in that same moment. And whether you recognize the deception or not, it knew how to start the devalue process. **Now what detains your joy retains your bondage.**

See your liberation is not always determined by what you don't do. However, it stands its ground, by what you choose to submit to.

Remember: one wrong consideration can cause an everlasting effect on your liberation.

It should always be our goal to be free. But when we are trapped in these selections, what should be, is hardly a reality. When you start feeling the pressure that comes with making major decisions, be vigilant, and sober that you will not devoured. **If you are not careful, you will numb your pain with temporaries. Be careful you don't become addicted to abusing**

yourself. Temporaries more than often terminate future.
1. The caretaker in the bedroom- but no joy
2. Over indulger in substance- but no joy
3. Religious activities- but no joy
4. Emotional withdrawal from people that really love you – but no joy

All this comes with improper selections.

Remember: what detains your joy- retains your bondage

My friend, it is our aggravations, which come from our selections, which give access to our attachments. I am not trying to get in your business. How many times were your selections reactive? We do it all the time. I don't mean any harm. We take these mental- emotional- physical-financial- and yes spiritual hits/hurts and then base your selections, and decisions AROUND THEM. Now the aggravations become acquainted with the vulnerability. There are too many times we make these declarations of devotion to ourselves, only to discover they have been violated by our temptations. (TRAPPED)

We take on this boldness with our mouth, but it results in a decline in our actions, thereby introducing us to a weakness, we never realize we had. So when we look at it from this perspective: we realize, that **it's not the pain of the person, but the misdirected passion that stems from me.** Don't deceive yourself.

My friend, it is not necessarily who you choose that is misdirected, but because of how you choose-and when you choose- and why you choose- and from where-and what emotion you choose them out of. Why you may ask? Normally how you choose, aids in who you choose. We attract who we are more than often. **The moment you start your selection based off hurt or history, you harm what should or could be healthy.** I don't mean any harm. The inability to select with stableness; could set you up for

43

delusion, destruction, and even devastation. Here is the dilemma. The standards, boundaries, expectations, and objectives are limited. I told you to pray. When we chose not **TO PRAY FOR THE RIGHT SELECTION, WE SELECT TO BECOME THE RIGHT PREY.**
You better have some combative skills (some fight). If you fail to prepare, you are preparing yourself for the fall. Please get this! **Not only is your weakness part of their comprehension, it also becomes their opportunity. People can tell when you have no fight, because everything they seem to throw; is never met by your resistance. It is called "easy access."** When there is no resistance, then there is no appreciation, or becomes lack of appreciation, it will bring the relationship to an ultimate destruction. The question is still on the floor. Is this a Relationship or a Relation trap? Can I help?
Quit looking for a positive outcome, while continuously accepting negative intakes. Once you come to the realization that my life matters, victimization will lesser in your reality.

Once again, decision-making:
1. Should I stay?
2. Should I go?
3. Should I return? Tricks- Traps- Truth
None of these are about my answer; however is totally about your attentiveness.
If you do not decide to promote& produce positivism in your selections, then you permit the penalty that comes with the choice. Have you ever discovered how the lion devours his prey?

There is usually three forms of devouring:
1. He catches them away from the pack(no one to hold you accountable)
2. He catches them wounded and licking the wounds(concentration on the past hurt)
3. He catches them in their immature stage(remember this stage you are intrigued, but not ready

My friend, understand when you are bound by these, you have now entered into a Relation trap. I don't mean any harm. The lion knows: by way of your indecisiveness "what's for dinner." It is seasoned just like they want you; undecided but anxious.

Be careful! We become so consumed, with the idea of having a relationship, that the concentration and proper observation is not intact. **We normally get consumed of by our own ignorance. Ignorance is always the bait used to draw our devourer closer.** Please remember: most times we believe that we are ready. So just like the buck, we leave stability for unsure. The lion needs you to think like this. Let me pause! We think like this: "I can handle me." **The stability can represent your progression, while the uncertainty is what creates your danger.** The progression comes into play, by the incremental steps necessary to make a healthy relationship. See my friend, entering in calls for progression, while you are in, it must produce the same. That is the essence & sign of growth, which develops the relationship. Here is the trap! When you are hesitant, but attempt it anyway. It's nothing wrong with believing. There is a point beyond believing…it's called knowing.

Curiosity most times will not prioritize. It only deals in the moment. What you consider in the moment of decision making, could be very well be the moment of delusional malfunctioning.

I told you the lion (the devourer) knows when you are out of place. People know when you are dislocated. What makes you easy prey is your inability to remain stable, because of your curiosity. I do not mean any harm. Just as the lion depends, people depend on you to think and act like this. Let me ask you a question. How long will you remain off course with your decision-making? How long will you halt between two decisions? Either you want a positive one, or you keep accepting the negative ones that come before you. **Without a solid understanding of your options; you will keep relinquishing golden opportunities, only to keep becoming your own obstacle. If not careful, delusional fantasies become nothing more than failed opportunities.** Here is the problem! We without awareness take on the weight of another person's stressful, chaotic, and painful world; then mix it with your unstable world, then expect a stable relationship. Remember: we help our hurt, progress our pain, and even embrace our embarrassments. Now look at the set up!

We become either:
1. **Confused**
2. **Abused**
3. **Or reused**

Now the stigma has created a repeated cycle that did not heal from the last one; and you are found licking your wounds, and the lion knows it. Now there is the residue mixed from the last+ the fresh hurt now= relation trap

Can I help? We put so much concentration on licking our wounds that in our licking session we forget to guard our minds. **Be careful that the concentration on the last hurt, does not neglect the detection of what could be hazardous now! THIS is BIG…THINK.**

I am talking to you. Because of no detection, your weakness is about to be overpowered by their strength. Have you notice how the lion catches his prey, attending to its wound forgetting to get in a safe place until healing. Now the lion that finds the prey licking the wound is not the one who caused it. However, because of easy access they are going to add to it, or finish you off. All around the world: there are desponded, broken and people filled with despair who did not find a place for healing. So in their limited understanding, they open themselves back up for more pain. The sad part about it is they set themselves up for the hurt, all over again. Just in case you did not know, and just in case I failed to tell you,

Your selection is vital!!! TAKE A MINUTE, AND PAUSE.

Please do not forget: people will not treat you with importance, if you do not make it as mandatory.

Remember: as long as we don't understand ourselves; we will become submissive to a definition that contradicts your original design.

Let's look at common mistakes:

- Destructive decisions- desperate decisions- delusional decisions
- Anxious answers
- Consistent confusion
- Bewildered- baffled behaviors

Something has to change!!!

What a bold statement. "Something has to change." I do not mean any harm. It is not a thing; it is always who. Now the question in your case: who has to change? This may depend on the severity of the challenge.

What is the challenge?

Here it is: Do I start?

1. Do I stay?
2. Do I re-enter?
3. Do I go?

My friend, the common denominator in all the questioning is I. That means you. It's time for some changing to be done.

Be careful! When we apply a behavior change, to produce an outcome, we too often misdirect our focus towards the outcome versus the change. **Sometimes change is needful and necessary, and not negotiable. The more you contemplate it, the more things can will become complicated.**

If it does not happen, the state of your wound will open itself wider, and the perplexity of thought only generates more pain.

I believe the power of your change only will comes with the presence of the challenge.

Therefore, here is the next challenge:

1. **How do you see your selection in the future?**
2. **What constitutes the value for this particular selection?**
3. **Why stay with that selection?**
4. **Is there any commonality with what you have chosen?**
5. **Are there mutual feelings involved?**

1 **BIG ONE- If you had not chosen them, would they have chosen you?**

You know I would not do you any harm. Some of our choices were not from a balanced consideration. However, they belong to an unstable desperation. Therefore, we start working overtime to fulfill the idea of having a relationship, never arriving to the fact that it is really non-existent. The question is still on the floor, relationship or relation trap. If you are calling for change, let it begin in you.

How can we do this?

Here is a list:

1. No longer can we make ourselves responsible for their: feelings, thoughts, decisions, behaviors, and even growth

48

2. You must stop trying to fix their feelings, to fit your world
3. No longer can you posture yourself to suffer their wanted consequences
4. No longer can you substitute it with your delusions, and call it your destiny

Remember: some have no clue how to treat you. If you have to train how to treat you, the relationship may already be in trouble.

One of the biggest indictments on relationships is lack of effort or evidence that both persons are participating. You can often tell lopsided relationships; when fatigue has set in, and the relationship is frequently camouflage by hope. There is consistency that comes with introspection, before you enter- after you enter or you're wanting to an exit. The pain that comes with negligence, will forever be prevalent in your reflection of what is considered as a successful relationship.

Be careful, that you don't start suffering from what you anticipated as a savior it could fail. You may find yourself; never acquiring what you desire and what you deserve. **So often, we become addicted to the anticipation, only to find it does not conclude in their decision making. Do not become guilty of being obligated to the person, and disloyal to yourself.** They will have you trying to fix something, while they work hard at keeping it broke. To keep finding yourself in these predicaments must mean one thing. **Your addiction has overruled your restrictions.**

I told you: the rules we often make, we extend the opportunity for people to break.

Look at the restrictions:

- **All visitors must sign in- which represent permission- too often they don't get access they take over and we allow them**
- **Be prepared to stop- because you don't stop the damage, they will not stop their delivery**

- Under construction- we too often forget this personal rule and take on another relation, only to be broken again
- Detour - the sadness that comes with this one- is when they start going the other direction, our desperation holds them up, and extends the trap

Dr. Larry Crabbs says: *"history has direction"*. In other words…. There are some old habits, behaviors, actions, and even attitudes that has been a part of you so long, it dictates the direction in which you go every time, and every relation trap. The reason why these traps are so prominent and dominating, they take on a direction and on a form that has not been sanctioned by God, but helps you, to keep experiencing these temporary satisfactions. **RIGHT HERE! HEALTHY VULNERABILTY IS NECESSARY**. What is that? That is the very thing that holds you at a place of self-regard, and self-care, and even self-respect- that you have discernment, but also a need for self-accountability.

REMEMBER:

- Who we pick
- How we pick
- Why we pick
- Where we pick
- What state do we pick them in
- When we pick

This is vital!

The #1 reason people are attracted to your weakness; is because of your **"panic picking"**

Challenge - QUIT PROMOTING THEIR POSSIBILITIES, through YOUR PANIC PICKS!!!!

My friend, **you will never acquire peace, when you inquire (request) chaos**. You are making a chaotic move; when we don't properly, select (take your time). We find ourselves looking for acceptance, when it may not be a present reality. Listen: you cannot mistake this for happiness. This may only be a momentary state of mind. We cannot misinterpret the content of the endeavors on their part. I believe the reason we do this, is because the limited options we pose to ourselves. **So a brighter future becomes a bargain, by a temporary fix.** This is what is sad; when we bargain our future, we really help produce the inevitable. What is the inevitable? Any relationship birth out of confusion and or chaos is doomed for destruction. The best thing you will then have is a hope. I am sorry! We need truth. Truth it is the only thing that will set you free.

Am I talking to you! You know you deserve a better future than what you have presently, or have had previously, or want to have now. But your silence needs a reality check. You keep putting proper thinking on hold, affirming it by foolishness.

You remember: something has to change.

Write here: one change needed

Let me ask you some questions:
1. When will the change happen?
2. How& Why is this change is necessary?
3. Where does the change need to take place?
4. What kind of change do you need to experience?
5. What are you driven by?
6. What gives birth to your conclusions

Hey! Are you listening? We must stop formulating these preventions in our minds, which we know will not work, because we know our delusions control the majority of our output.

Stop Here! Make a List
1. What has been my normal tolerances- (what have I put up with)
2. What have been their mistakes/ mine

51

3. What adjustment do I need to make NOW
4. What things I have not prayed about- before entering- during- or possible exit

You might want to close the book; this represents accountability. I found most people occasionally will rebel, reject, or reduce the knowledge of something or someone that will cause them to think pass their stimulation, and cause them to look at PERSONAL evaluation. See it's in our stubbornness we extract ourselves out the contribution we added to the problem. Not realizing that there may be surface problems, but there are root causes.

Tim,

Can I talk to you? Seems as if the ability to extricate (free) my emotions, my mind my body, and even my spirit is becoming more of an assignment than expected. You have no clue: my love, my time, my loyalty, my respect will not disengage from this entanglement. The heartbreaking penalty is I can't seem to get loose; but what befuddles me is I do not want to be loose.

What is happening to me? Seems like I apply myself to habits that keep forming my responses.

 Sincerely, Just about to lose it....

Well, just about to lose it, I need you remember one thing. **We pick our pain or help our hurt.**

See what disallows the resentful emotions, corner us into believing we are responsible for the overwhelming feeling we have towards those who purposefully devour us. When you think you are emotionally, and psychologically, escaping from it: you find yourself encamped around it. **Is it a Relationship or Relation trap?**

Let pause and pray: Lord help me with proper decision-making. Amen

(Pause for minute) If I have not said this to you by now, let me do so. Trust in the lord with all your heart, and lean not to your understanding. But in all your ways acknowledge him; he will direct your path.

At this point in the book: you may not want to admit it, you have committed yourself to a dangerous need. It is the need to feel secure, or good about the selection you made, and the need for a co-signer.

Just be careful, in your choices, you do not become numb to wisdom. Too many times, I have encountered people that made rejection a normality. When you arrive here, self- destruction may be in the forecast, Here is a list:

1. You start ignoring problems- pretending there is none, and get mad at others who detect you have one
2. Telling or convincing yourself of a better tomorrow by trying the same old stuff – survey says- "0"
3. You watch problems get worse- but refuse to have a day with reality
4. Create an over indulgence due to abandonment

RIGHT HERE, I PUT IT BACK ON YOU- **STOP! YOU NEED SOMEBODY TO GET IT RIGHT, YOU NEED THEIR DILIGENCE, WHEN IT COMES TO LOVING YOU AND BEING IN RELATIONSHIP WITH YOU. WHILE ALL THESE EXPECTATIONS ARE IN PLAY, YOU TAKE THE LETHARGIC APPROACH.**

DO NOT FORGET YOU MUST LOVE YOURSELF, <u>WITH THE SAME ENERGY YOU PUT INTO YOUR EXPECTATION.</u>

I believe I hit a nerve. **People do not respect, and love you properly, because they recognize lack of respect, and love you have for yourself. Why you say that? I believe if you really love, and respected yourself; those people would not be granted access.**

53

Let me help! SELF SABOTAGE- The deliberate and damaging or destruction of self. Wow! YOU deliberately destroy yourself with these panic picks, and delusional desperations, that keep landing you in these relation traps.

What happens?

- **Dodging emotions**- you cannot avoid negative thinking
- **Procrastination** - the gap between intent and action- You keep putting off your sanity, for self-satisfaction. But it is sabotage. What you are doing, and what you meant to do are too often in far and between. You get lost in your deliberation, then try justify your delay for better
- **Take on the extreme modesty posture**- to the point of lack of confidence
- **Addictions**- keep trying to fix mistakes, by keep adding on increasingly bad choices

I found out: we may have to expose what has been comfortable externally (on the outside) to impose on what has been hiding internally (on the inside). It is not until you begin to dig that you really discover...

My friend, I have discovered the ability to encounter the magic of a productive relationship is controlling the artistry of loving yourself. Probably the main thing that must change; is how you see yourself, and how you allow others to see you. Do not be dictated by their discovery, neither their by your delusions.

Watch this! Without knowledge of their intentions, you just may be submitting your vulnerability and ignorance. Thereby, supplying them with weapons, that could wipe out any possibility of survival.

You really must be wise in this sense. Often times God has way of sending you necessary directions to catapult you into what is vital for your growth and even departure. However, because we are apt to reject, we are left without resolve.

Why is that Tim?

I believe that when advice is given, because it often does not bring instant gratification; that our common reaction is rejection. We are expecting people to like our choices, without their perception. And if they perceive that you are clueless to their intention, it could ignite a struggle with wisdom. We hasten to rejection; because truth enlightens and holds you accountable to what you know is wrong.

The bible stands clear: that a fool hates knowledge (instruction) and will not hear it. You see: **THE Rebellion that comes with the anxiety can make you almost equivalent to a fool.** Let me ask you a question. Have you ever paid any attention the characteristic of a fool?

Look at the list:

1. They hasten to decisions
2. They do not like correction, instruction on their opinion/ adherence to knowledge
3. Reject wisdom
4. The cling to comfort in their instability
5. Seem to revive contentions
6. Confusion has become necessary for their existence
7. Please look, and see if you are being pursued, or have you seized any of these.

If this is the case, you have to be more careful. **It is what we try to hide that becomes an extension to our hurt.**

You know I am right. The things you should be getting away from, is the very thing you like to stay around.

Tim you are right!!! I hate it; but love it at the same time. Separation would be easy, but the indulge want allow me to break away. You say, "I don't like it" but find yourself wanting more of it. At this point listen to BIG MAMA "Can't tell you nothing with your hard head".

Something has to change!
If not careful, you will find yourself obligated to the obsession of having a relationship. All this comes with the lack of recognition that you are in a trap. The reason departure now becomes dismal, is the desire that comes with the addiction. It is has become such a preferred bondage that you cannot, and you will not break away. I don't mean any harm. **You become loyal, to the very thing that causes you to be disloyal to yourself.** **I forgot to love myself. Oh wretched man that I am.** This dejected stage is a direct result of improper selections. Can I help? The answer to your problem is not always another relationship. In your quest to resolve the matter, you may have just found the addition to your problem. The fact is that individuals have problems, which are not all conquered through romanticism. I do not mean to criticize. But normally after the moment of romanticism, comes the enduring skepticism. Now what you considered a romantic incline has become a revolting decline.

NOW AT THIS POINT:
1. ADMIT YOUR PART
2. APOLOGIZE TO YOURSELF
3. ABUSING YOURSELF MUST BE A THING OF THE PAST

Tim I am trying to get away!
Here is the problem. **You are trying to get away from the individual physically...when you mentally and emotionally keep them. So in body they are gone, but psychologically they yet remain.** Be careful! This may hinder any other relations that you may encounter. Why you may ask? **When you do not rid yourself of what was; what could be will forever seem unattainable.** Please do not miss this! **Detachment is not separating from the person whom we care about. However, it is getting out of the misery of the attachment. What make it so**

56

intense; is that I am trying to stay devoted, to very thing that has never really been attached to me.

If you feel like you are losing it... uncomfortable may be better at this point!

The Cycle has to be broken!

- **Unknown existence of the relationship**
- **Different person same spirit**
- **Uncomfortable feelings(something just aint right)**
- **Panic picking**
- **Unpleasant truth- this one is no good**

My friend, I have found out most of us seek to obtain knowledge about our picks, while ignoring the tradition and truths about ourselves. When we refuse or reject the fact; that we need to break the cycle of dysfunction, we rid ourselves of authenticating a productive relationship.

One writer said, (Tim Grier) "It is not that they push you down, you extended the invitation to be shove." If this is the case, then why do we cry about our <u>CHOSEN</u> posture?

Is this a relationship or a relation trap?

Remember: you are responsible for the outcome. You cannot pretend anymore. We must ascertain the need for change. The present moment is only producing a way of acceptance and or reality. When we started out, I conveyed that this would not be a book on the manipulation of choice, but accountability. It was to promote a level of responsibility back to yourself.

 So you must BREAK THE CYCLE!!!!!

C- ONSEQUENCES

Y-OU

C-OMMIT TO

L-EARN-love lust

E- Energize

S- for self-satisfaction

Am I in the right one? Do I need to come out of this one? Shall I go in another one?

All these are valid questions. You are responsible for making conscious choices. Understand for so long, the concentration has been the other person. Watch this! **It is not based off another individual's performance; it is your reaction after they have performed.** What causes you to create a mess, stay in a mess or become a mess, it is the lack of accountability not to entertain your demise.

Can I help? **What you chose not to dry up, you unintentionally drown in. Now what was a tear has become your flood.**

Am I talking to you? The proclivity of not cleaning up your mess will spill over into your regret. Some times yesterday, carry so much capacity, that the burdens of trying to move on, start over or either stay in leave you clueless. Let me ask those who have been mesmerize by vicissitudes of these past relation traps, who did it?

Who- how – when- where- why- what?? ? ?

If you were left dangling, somebody left you there.

They didn't believe in you recovery skills

1. They left you to die in yesterday
2. They had already counted you out at their expense
   I need to know who did it.
3. Who married you; and then mess your life up?
4. Who abandon you with those kids?
5. Who broke camp after all resources were depleted?
6. Who decided to take your love for granted?
7. Who thought their cheating would charm you?
8. Who drained you – spiritually- mentally- emotionally- psychologically- and yes financially?

Ok my friend, we are not going to pretend that it did not happen.

What happened did happen- what was said, they said it- how you are feeling, it is for real.

Listen, **your uniqueness has to be more than your weakness.** If you are going through this selection phase be

58

ready. You must be prepared to be flexible and concrete. These things must come with your selection as well as coping mechanisms. You may not feel that is mandatory to leave, but there must be some stability if you plan on staying.

Please know this: confusion cannot meet confusion and expect stability.

Hey, there are a few things, I need you to get before we move on.

1. if you are going back in, **go with caution**
2. if you are coming out, **know it with assurance**
3. if you are staying in , **stay with confidence, not with reserves**

Whatever the case; **YOU CAN DO IT!!!!**

This time make sure it is a Relationship, and not a Relation Trap

The impact of yesterday creates an impatience for today, destroying the importance for tomorrow.

You cannot be ignorant to the devices of what you have learned. This time of engagement has not been for my exercise. However, to challenge you in the place of your personal execution.

When people educate you about them, please believe them. If we are going to excel in real relationships, we cannot evade nor ignore the warnings of a relation trap.

ARE YOU STRONG ENOUGH TO BREAK THE BEHAVIOUR AND THE CYCLE? WHAT CYCLE? THE ONE THAT KEEPS DRIVING YOU TO PANIC PICK. DON'T ALLOW THE ENEMIES CALLED: STUPIDITY- IGNORANCE- OR HURT DESTROY YOUR CHANCES OF A POSITIVE- PRODUCTIVE AND PRIVILEDGE RELATIONSHIP!

I know you don't want to be alone; but creating more painful problems, will only substitute, and never satisfy. **Be careful not to minimize your pain, while maximizing**

your panic! If you fail to listen, you may very well forsake your learning. Now what could have a permanent change in your behavior tendency, could disrespectfully ignore the experience. The visible manifestations of your crisis will show up in every negative selection, and everything you do.

If it says:

Do not enter- guess what

Slow down- you had better take your time

Under construction- learn how to wait

Dead in road- you better know what pre-caution means

Remember:

When you chose to ignore, you also chose to ignite.

Relationships must be exposed to individualism, and uniqueness for survival. The absenteeism of either one, leaves delusion and self- damage. The more you depend on others without accepting the uniqueness that God has place in you; it could cause depreciation to be more obvious.

You have every right to enter in a positive relationship

You have every right to come out of a negative one

You have every right to enjoy the one you are previously in

But it is according to the power that is at work in you.

12 Rules to the selection phase

Don't forget these:

1. **Know it is necessary to detach from disorder**
2. **Know if is time to re- introduce yourself**
3. **Do not approve dysfunctions**
4. **Know how to detect unstableness and underdevelopment**
5. **Manufacture your own healing without a co-dependency**
6. **Do not disregard the re-occurrence of cycles and your re-enforcement to certain patterns**

7. Make sure your picks are stable and settled, not surrendered
8. Be educated on the person- and re-evaluate your weakness
9. Maintain order and competence
10. Do not fail the assurance test
11. Be cautious when disbelief keeps arriving/ what you are experiencing could be actual what is real.
12. You always have a better choice.
13. As long as we fail to administer behaviors, that would advance our essentials; we will continue to intensify our detriments.
    Staying too late Or Leaving too soon starts with how you select

CHAPTER 2

THE IMPATIENT & LONELY STAGE

I am back!!!!
Let's look at this word <u>impatience.</u>
Synonymous with:
1. Agitation-
2. anxiety- irritability
3. nervousness-
4. restlessness-
5. quick temper
6. snappy
7. edginess
8. hasty – out all these; can you declare that's me?-(look at the list)
All these are link to one word; and it is called **impatience.**
Oh, my friend get ready for a mind-blowing experience, as we explore this disease called "impatience."
 When we look at the words above, we can discover that even though they are synonymous, they are also symptoms.
DEFINE- I CAN NOT WAIT- PLEASE HURRY!! Now Impatience:

1. the lack of patience
2. Eager desire for relief or change; restlessness.
3. intolerance of anything that thwart, delay, or hinders

"The Hurry up Me"

This word is put into action, more than any other word in most relation traps; and is the cause of hurt in most relationships. Love – trust- faith- honesty-patience- takes a back seat when this word is in action. Why you must ask? It is never willing to wait; it must have a now resolve, and a now answer. Impatience will always show itself irritable, edgy, nervous, and restless. Because the idea of being put on hold, the idea of process and progression is illogical. Why can't we just start the relationship, and worry about everything later? Can I help? **Most of your improper selections (chap 1) are born out of intensified impatience. Because the majority of impatient people, will always personalize the intensity. So yes, you can have a trap with the lingering impatience, but never a real relationship.**

__Charles Caleb Colton says "patience is the support of weakness; impatience is the ruin of strength."__

We place such an emphasis on a quick fix, the idea of putting some time into the potential seems null and void. Tim what do you mean? I mean that because we have a history of failure, whether it is our fault or someone else's, we become more apt to try it again without proper investigation and evaluation. Let me say this: most times we have to re- enter or walk away from it… because no one took the time to realize this one is not the one. So we devote a TREMEDOUS AMOUNT of unnecessary time, trying to camouflage for others and convince them, with false reality of our own. Watch this! **Because of the intensity that comes with this mindset, we set ourselves up for multiple disappointments. Our multiple**

disappointments, lead us into multiple failures. Our failures give strength to our crisis, and our impatience to find a resolve within ourselves. We seemly become conditioned to this pattern, that our impatience has become our stronghold. I don't want to offend. **Our need to increase pleasure, and reassurance that we have a relationship, aims to reduce our discomfort; that it is not. Your unwillingness to detect this trap, overrules the opportunity to think & believe otherwise. Be careful!!!** You may be sending the wrong message. What is that? I am impatient. **Now what you were not willing to wait on, as time permits places a greater weight on you. <u>Your anxiety often creates assumption. Your assumption; is never concrete, but will assist you, with your indecisiveness.</u>**

How can you have anything positive or productive if you are uncertain?

My friend, once you introduce them to the impatient& lonely you, all attributes you wish to add is now impeded. Your impatience could be interpreted as fear, and use for their manipulation. This is why you have to be careful. Whatever the case may be; it can ruin longevity in the relationship, but linger in a relation trap. Are you ready for this? This type of behavior can disable the true you. **Is it a relationship or a relation trap?** Not allowing the maturation to take place, will always find you settling for what is not suitable. You will begin to battle with competence and also begin to bargain with clarity. Thereby, leaving you in a compromising position.

Big mama can you help me? **"Get somewhere and sit down".**

Along with this presentation, and what you need them to comprehend; there is a clash with compatibility and even commonality. Therefore, at the time of meeting, you have perceived that you are in a relationship. I am sorry! You have been deceived into wrong thinking, **it is a trap.**

65

Impatience carries a satisfaction, which will increase outer conflicts, and will limit inner convictions. Watch out!
If you are in so much of a hurry, they will permit you to be. The relationship will not have any life to it. The intentions in the initial phase of the relationship; will be concealed if your impatience dominates them. I found the more the relationship progresses, the more the symptoms can become evident. **Remember: that impatient people are intense people. Either we are controllers of impatience or we are contributors to it.** I believe that impatience is a form of a tantrum. Tantrums are things that need immediate attention. That is how impatience acts: **it always needs/requires/ and request a right now fix.** This is a direct result of low acceptance& high tolerance. Either we accept tantrums or we have them. The dilemma with this: there is no clarification on your priorities. When you start branding approval on what is inappropriate; it gladly receives its validation through your anxiety.
Let me ask you a few questions:
Are you ready to go in?
Do you need to come out?
Is this one the one?
Remember: *"To thy own self be true." (Shakespeare)*
People will know what is necessary, but will only accommodate you based on your frustration. **Your frustration (symptom) does not hold them accountable. However, it makes you less responsible.** Am I talking to you? It is your impatience that helps intensify your imperfections. So they didn't have to limit you during the relationship; the introductory of your limitations were there from the beginning. Tim are you asking me to be perfect? No of course not, I am encouraging you to be cautious. **Your frustration right here can/will activate your assumption. Thereby, nourishing the anxiety.**

One of our biggest problems; is we have not found a remedy to the "gotta have it" attitude. The "Hurry up Me" neglects clarifying due to the desperation. **You cannot command what you do not commit to yourself.** Now discovering this, you will be back where you claimed you would never be. **Once again, you want them to commit to you, when you are not committed to yourself. The idea of starting over or even letting go is not based off experience, but competency. "Do you know where you are going to? Do you like the things life is showing you?" Do you know?**

LET ME ASK YOU A QUESTION.

When will you start promoting something, or producing something positive, and productive through yourself, and for yourself?

When will you stop penalizing yourself because the lack of patience?

It's your anxiety that needs a resolve. If not, it is suddenly absorbed by a "quicker fixer upper."

It is in our moments of hesitation that we turn to meaningless attachments. This may be a strong indication, that I may not be engaged into a patient way of thinking. There must be a resolve. Whether you believe it or not; the right interactions, at the wrong time will encourage these negative attachments, and also aid in the wrong expectations. My friend, don't miss this. Making a quick decision, without solidarity and validity, sets you up for another trap, and another failed relationship. The sad thing: it's happening simultaneously as you are in your delusional stage.

There is couple of things to put in your bag:

1. **The death of bad relationships occur when I wake up to the reality… I need patience.**
2. **The things you are overly anxious about are the very thing that causes the most frustration.**

3. The problem is we do not train ourselves, to recognize our impatience; that's why irrational decisions keep on haunting us.

My friend, people look and lurk for your perceived loneliness. It is in your weakness, that your impatience can rob you of longevity. This time of your life, should be preparing you. Nevertheless, so often it does not prepare you, it prevails over you. **Warning!!!** When you refuse to wait, be patient, take your time, you can easily embrace you future embarrassments; and construct another world of emptiness.

Tim you don't understand. **I understand that we constantly extend our loneliness into lustful moments**. You find these temporaries; who can only fulfil temporary. Then you find yourself void again. Sorry! **We have these permanent delusions with a temporary destiny.** I understand it is your greed to fulfill the need. Here is the sadness and the madness; after the lustful moment, it transports you back to loneliness. Why do you say that? Have you ever been in a hurry, got what you perceived to be it, and then felt empty because you knew it had to be more than just a feeling. **Now the very thing, that initially energized your feeling, now is exasperating your future.**

I do not mean any harm. In your refusal to be patient, you went wandering, not realizing you were weakening at the same time. Now any potential move that would have seem to appear positive may never get a chance to be in operation due to your eagerness.

I have learned in my life, when you become impatient, you forget what is important.

Let's look at the rundown:
1. I became impatient
2. I forgot that I was important
3. My impatience brought about such an impact

4. Now the impact left the impairment of self –worth even more obvious
5. I realize the impairment has impeded my growth, my trust and even my health

Now you have been imposed on by somebody who knew you were impatient, knew your less importance, knew they would have an impact, and knew the impairment of your choices would impede your outcome. How do I know? Because these are the consequences, that packages itself with impatience.

Be careful! These impressions intrigues the impulse; causing impotency in every potential, and great relationship.

Oh my friend, did you catch that?

Because you did not wait, could not wait, would not wait; practicing a healthy, prosperous relationship does not seem applicable. Be careful! What is not practiced, will start to affect, and infect your thought pattern. Thereby, causing you to move or jump unwisely. Now the association will reap the effects of being powerless and ineffective.

1. Why do you keep experiencing failure?
2. Why is it they don't last
3. Why do I give so much and get so little?

Answer: impatience will always control your initial feeling. However, will never feel obligated to introduce the real facts. The consideration of truth and the obligation to facts is an anesthesia to impatience. Sorry! The failures you have been experiencing, may be an inevitable, and a direct result of unwanted evidence.

Loneliness- why me

Why do I keep attracting the same old type? Who do you normally attract? Pause- consider- write them down. DO not leave anyone out-

Here is the answer. Most instances; we are who we attract. We proclaim not to be, but we are. We keep drawing what

69

we like, because in essence that is how we are. I know you are a nice girl, who likes the hardcore man. However, behind the pretty, nice mask resides the hardcore woman. That is why we do not move away; and they keep drawing nigh. All this is based upon your level of loneliness. Your level of loneliness intersects with impatience and they both will contribute to your downfall.

Remember this: **loneliness and impatience only remedy is "I gotta have it right now."**

CAN I HELP?

If they don't earn you; then do not freely offer yourself. The reason why there is a continuation of failures, and flops in our relations is the force of loneliness. The pressure that comes with fighting the temptation, routinely becomes effortless. Reason being: is that loneliness will always chat with impatience, to create a plan. **Now your plan is to reap the benefits; not realizing you have just perpetuated your detriments.**

Why do we give people access? Not just access, but free access, who are not willing to work for the relationship. This could be the reason you are encountering these relation traps.

Watch this! Now the relationship is no longer an opportunity, it has become an option.

Tim I told you. What is so wrong with me? I keep telling myself it is so good to me and for me; but in essence I know it's not for me. **When you fail to properly prepare yourself; you will continually have to repair yourself.**

Yes, I hate the fact of how they do me, but I love the fact it is them that is doing it.

Tim, loneliness and impatience has a hold on me. That may be true; but you had better get of hold of yourself.

Some of us have not learned the art of being alone. We have allowed it to co-exist, or define it as loneliness. That's why we have been bombarded with anxiety. It would be one thing if the impulsive character would stop; but the

70

stubbornness that presents itself with impatience disallows it. Watch this! Repeatedly you are fighting with your impulse, and time after time, you are on the losing end. Why is that Tim? Well, is not that you are not putting up a fight; you just keep putting down your guard. **There is such a failure in our emotional intelligence; that we don't monitor, and we fail to maintain.**
Tim what is really going on?
Let us see:
1. What use to be just a simple feeling has turned into an overwhelming sensation
2. Sometimes our vision is obscured by our conditions
3. Your responses vary because they have become learned responses
4. You find yourself trying to maintain a perfect fantasy. Thereby, leaving you irresponsible to the reality.

Can I help?
1. **How good it is, does not determine what is best for you.**
2. **The externals feature, does not always guarantee an everlasting future**
3. **How much they spent, will never determine how much time they willing to spend.**

Remember: The impact of yesterday, the impatience of today can be your ruins for tomorrow.
It's when you have encountered, and experienced, so many weak and wounded moments that the anticipation of something new, something different is unbelievable. Some of your anxiety is aligned with your belief system. You do not believe better, so you impatiently accept anything. *"Whether you think you can or you can't you are right." (Henry ford)*
Tim Grier- "Your can't starts out verbal, until it becomes visible."

I told you; that contemplation and ignorance often hangs out together. We create these pathologies of failures, due to our interpretation of loneliness

Now the very thing we altered will in return adjust your future. Remember: fantasy does not secure future. **Have you ever considered the fact, that impatience does not require dedication?** My friend, one of the main reasons for unsuccessful relationships is the hurry up me attitude. I am sorry. There can be no credibility extended to this pattern of unsuccessful thinking. Let me ask you a question. **Are you so impatient, that you are willing to expose someone else to your struggles, for the sake of another relation trap?**

By now, you ought to be exhausted from the relation traps; that KEEP providing no wins, and too many loses. Here is the dilemma: it is not about how they treated you, but how impatiently we have treated ourselves.

This is the wavering process intensifies. Because it is in your wavering that we may increase our unstableness. Remember: A double man is unstable in all his ways. See the unwillingness to patiently wait, hinders positive relational production. If you are edgy, irritated, agitated, quick tempered, restless, you might want to check your patience level and growth.

Look at the some things to try:
1. Keep your true self in charge
2. Maintain a genuine mutual respect (common respect) do not do all the work
3. Give clarity on your needs, feelings, and rights
4. Have Fluency(confidence) in the relationships – skills and awareness- assertion

Tim, all this sound good; I just do not have time to practice it. Did you know that even impracticability can navigate through your impression? Help me understand! We make having a positive/ productive relationship impossible. It starts first in your mind, then the impatience re- directs and

strategize the route, it needs you to take. Now after the plan is in place; your thoughts your ideas, intuition, and feelings will be censored. How you should think and feel, is now being replaced with the "hurry up you." Watch out that your mind don't become conducive for impatience. All it needs to know that you are not willing, and will not try, and without hesitation have already accepted. WARNING!!!
I brought a few friends along who would love to help:

1. Alexander Dumas Pere (French writer)- "All human wisdom is summed up in two words- wait and hope"
2. Saint Augustine (Christian Theologian)- "Patience is the companion of wisdom"
3. Leo Nikolaevich Tolstoy (Russian Novelist)- " the two most powerful warriors are patience and time"
4. Benjamin Franklin- "He that can have patience can have what he will"
5. Ralph Waldo Emerson (American Poet)- "Patience and fortitude conquers all things"
6. Tim Grier says through the word of God; they that wait on the Lord shall renew their strength.

Will you allow me to keep it real with you; some of our main reasons why we do not stay, need to leave, or fail to have a productive one, is we do not wait on God. We worry, but will not wait. When we fail to become sensitive to where we are…it can possibly leave us senseless.

Let us think:
1. Try to remain positive and anticipate the best
2. What you are waiting on must is accompanied by-sound judgment, clear understanding, and knowledge of the very thing that has your attention
3. You have developed combative skills against those things that make me think, act, irrationally. That time and chance happens to us all.

4. Governing myself to wait, affords me the opportunity to have success in what I believed
With this resolution and strength I can triumph over all things
5.All of it comes with understanding; it is God, who holds the key to my strength and with my patience, I am being restored. As I renew my thinking, I then can restore right relationship.

See my friend, the introspection of who you are, and how you think, will set a new perspective on relationships. Can I help? **Until proper examinations accompany us, we will continue to experiment and not properly execute.**
If there will be another perspective, we will have to look at it from some different angles to help aid in this process.

Let us look:
1. Scientific perspective-In evolutionary psychology-(the study psychological adaptation in your physical and social environment), these are the things that can affect- memory, perception, and even your language. It says patience is studied as a decision-making problem, involving the choice of either a small reward in the short term, or a more valuable reward in the long term. **Tim says** the problem with us; is that we would not even dignify this concept of having a valuable long term relationship. Why? It signifies that it would be a process in doing so. The hurry up you; does not have time for this. So instead of receiving what is best, <u>impatience </u>will accept a consolation prize. Now the self –control paradigm in which you have to choose, now is in place. **Do I**

choose right now? Do I wait for later? Impatience says nowwww!!!

2. Religious perspective - That patience and fortitude (strength and endurance in a painful situation) are prominent themes- another extols that patience as an important trait. That even though you may suffer challenging conditions; you can still endure until you are rescued from it. It is stated in Proverbs; "A patient man is better than a warrior, and he that rules his temper, than he who takes the city. It warns us not to become quickly discontented, for it lodges in the bosom of a fool. Patience is also known as one most valuable virtues of life. Here is my question to you. **WHY do we fail to embrace THIS VIRTUE?** Here is the answer: there is no self-control over our anxiety, and this what keeps impatience alive. Thereby, causing our discontent, our quick temper, irrational beliefs and unstable decisions, that cause the impact of our consequences, leaving damage as our reality. **SELF AWARENESS TIME!!!!**

I told you; the reason internally we are so frustrated is because in most relation traps we are only driven by external features. **Once again features do not secure futures.** We are in such a rush, that we become unaware of the potency that comes along with these traps. So many times when undetected, your eagerness can, and will magnify the cycles.

Cycles...
C- CONSEQUENCES
Y- YOU
C- COMMIT TO
L- learn- love-LUST
E- ENERGIZES- FOR
S-SELF -SATISFACTION

See my friend, before it became a habit- it was thought- but after the thought, you became committed to the action. **I believe impatient actions; are habits in practice.** The problem is that the impatient behavior, intensifies the potential for it to become a normal way of thinking and responding. When we fail to recognize it's a trap, then the trap successfully satisfies and deters you from a real relationship. So the initial warnings; are no longer available or accessible to you. It is your rejection and denial that intercepts the chance of what could be or what is deserving. The freedom that comes with authentic relationships; has now been transformed into bondage. Why you say that? **It is because things you lusted after, in your impatience, will now render consequences you never anticipated.** I don't mean any harm this is the pattern of impatient people. They fail to execute certain thought and patterns, which would exclude certain behaviors, never breaking the cycle of defeat or the dysfunction that comes with it. **My friend, when we refuse to break this cycle, that keeps you in bondage, it's the same cycle that numbs us to change. THINK!** You can better yourself. **SAY IT! I CAN BETTER MYSELF.** Discovery is not enough, determination must follow. What do you mean? YOU have to see that transformation is available. You do not have settle. THERE is someone WHO really loves you for you. THEY want a right relationship. Now you must be determine to have it. **If you study long...you might study wrong.**

Question?

When was the last time you took inventory of the traps you continually fall into? **OKAY LETS PAUSE AND IDENTIFY YOUR WEAKNESS LIST (WRITE THEM)**
1.You have to be careful, not to become so routine that you become too relaxed. You still need to maintain competence and discretion. Just in case I did not mention; IMPATIENCE OFTEN EXPOSES YOUR VUNERALBILITY. Sometimes vulnerability is not when you are slumped over and weak; it comes as a result of relaxation without proper assurance AND completing the process. So many times we will be tempted in the area, we think we have conquered. Only to come to the realization; we did not pass the test. Your goal is always from start to finish; not from start to pause. If you do not train yourself to be disciplined, you will succumb to another cycle.

Believe me or not, your progress becomes laughter to the enemy. Why? The enemy always believes, that you don't believe.

It is in our impatience that after we conclude, and we realize, we did it without personal analysis of ourselves. It is not their activity that deters us. However, it's our failure to reject what has been offered, due to obliviousness that comes with impatience.

Remember:

What I am waiting on should be accompanied by sound judgment, clear understanding, and knowledge of the very thing that has my attention.

That I must develop some combative skills, against that which make me think or even act irrational.

We fail to face our true identity because of lack of perspective and perception. Impatience limits you on both. Once again, you can never take a thorough examination, if there is no proper execution. We must learn how to forgive ourselves. **STOP! SAY IT! I FORGIVE ME! SAY IT AGAIN!**

When we fail to do so, we cease to win against the internal struggles, which seemly plague us on a frequent basis. **My friend, it is one thing to blame yourself; it is another in forgiving yourself.**

Do me a favor and ask yourself these questions.

- Who am I?
- Why am I like this? Answer it with truth. Then hit restart.

I must encourage you that who you are, is not defined by people, situations, or even events. They mold and shape some character, but never should define the true essence of who you were created to be. It is in our impatience, that we miss our true essence. **Stop looking for radical change in people; before we discover the need for personal evaluation of ourselves.** Have you discovered in your quest; that you have only been attracting people, who really can't help you with true essence? Why do you say that? Because they would help lead you to true love, not just self-satisfaction. You don't have to be real with me. However, it seems like each time, they lead you to empty, and they leave full.

- You are empty on love- while they are full off your ignorance.
- You are empty on stability - while they are full on personal satisfaction

We pick our pain, and help our hurt, through our impatience. So we anticipate, with no education, nor investigation of the facts. We want transformation overnight; when in essence you did not get this way overnight. Hey! News FLASH "THEY DID NOT EITHER". People will do a temporary change, if it means they will eventually control your future sanity **if they detect that your impatience has led you to a place of stupidity; then they will camouflage their character just to control yours.**

I told you, you have trained people how to handle you. "I got myself together" vs. "I'm getting it together". It is when you are getting it together, THAT impatience does its best work. PLEASE KNOW THE DIFFERENCE. Sorry! But you have attempted to be in relationships with people; who depend on your impatience as mean of their survival. Why do you say? **Because if you ever get it together: they would not be a factor only a figment.** See, it is our rededication to return to our rightful state, that becomes even more awkward and agonizing but needful. Most of us are not dedicated to the complete operation of change.

- We start- but never allow the maturation of the change. We will get halfway then regress, because our progression is taking too long
- We become lazy- so effort has no chance
- We easily fall for desperation on our part- and deception on theirs

Dedication will never link itself to impatience. Dedication will always ask for persistence, while impatience will always require resistance. It is in our impatience that we create our inventory list. Our need of affection and belonging is left misconstrued due to our impatience. Here is the problem: as long as we essentially have what we call love and affection, our esteem is high. It is in the absence that we become non- existent, and more than often face self -abandonment. So the mindset that we partake in, causes us to counter act with irrational decision making.

WAKE UP!!! YOU WERE FEELING VALUABLE-CONFIDENT-AND EVEN SATISFIED UP TO THE DISAPPOINTMENT& LONLEY STAGE- NOW DISSAPPOINTMENTS SET IN,AND YOU DON'T FEEL ACCESSIBLE ANYMORE. **"BREAKING NEWS"**

TIM HAS COME TO GET YOU OUT OF THIS SLUMP!!!
LET'S PRAY! DEAR LORD, I NEED TO COME OUT OF THIS SLUMP, AND I THANK YOU FOR BRINGING ME OUT OF THIS SLUMP TODAY. AMEN!!!

See when the want is frustrated, that is when you start feeling inferior, weak, and even helpless. Here is the sad part: the situation that you keep putting emphasis on, does not add to your worth& value. **The more you add to it by worry, the more you subtract from your worth.** It is the impact of impatience that causes us not to outlast or overcome our SLUMP. **It is our emotions, and our perception that causes us to stay too late, or that causes us to leave too soon. The question is still vital; a relationship or a relation trap? If you are not careful failure will become an option- from an option to a practice- from a practice to a lifestyle- from a lifestyle to a numbness- and some cases from a numbness to designed delusion.**

Our instability keeps creating these opportunities to fail in relationships. Not only do we fear this pattern of defeat... we begin to doubt what we can accomplish. What I fail to accomplish by patience; is evident by my constant battle with anxiety. My inability to wait, becomes unwanted but an acceptable addiction. So for the sake of believing I have a relationship, I will find myself psychologically succumbing to an awaited trap.

Here is the normal acceptance list:
- Short term gratification- as long as I have something/someone
- Obsessive focus- without a realistic view
- The fantasy of the "perfect relationship" without the knowledge of the trap
- Retentive cycles of pain and dismay

- Periodic doubts - without levels of accountability

To tell the truth; we don't want it. But because there is no productive view of ourselves; impatience obliges us with an unproductive obscurity.

This is why loneliness hurt so severe. We allow another person to attach and dis-engage as they please. Thereby, approaching this emotion without the proper knowledge of managing your responses. This can be vital. See my friend, the problem is not, you didn't know them. You have not educated yourself concerning your improper reactions. Sometimes our impatience is a direct sign from our hurt/ rejections- and even our assumption.

Rejections: To refuse, to decline, to deny or to discard.

Everyone who enters into a relationship, enters in with the anticipation that it will be successful. No one go down aisles, say their vows, and spend years together looking to discover the inevitable of hurt and rejection. There is no way you projected, or detected this would be the end result. Now the question has to be; how do you respond- how to do I bounce back from this? I know this event, and the hurt is tampering with your sanity. Who in the right mind likes to be denied or discarded? I do understand that being denied happiness hurts. The effort and memory, even our energy put in to what we perceive as successful, often ends up promoting our next hardships. In worse case scenarios; this is being experienced on a day to day basis in present relationships. **Did I stay too late** or **did I leave too soon?** I know sometimes in our relationship, we are not privy to peace, to joy, and sanity that should come within the confines of a relationship.

Be careful! That you don't use hurt to hurt. We often use what we were hurt by, to hurt people with. So we begin to muster up the idea of repay, manipulation in our next relationship ventures. Because we fail to resolve the hurt, the only remedy we have is to do the same.

I want to take the time to apologize; to those who had to experience the impact of rejection. Those who were and are, being denied and discarded by someone who once you held in the highest regards. The tears and fears that has been the thorn in your production of positive relationships.

These things often plague your esteem as a person. Tim how do you know? It happen to me. **(My story coming up)** My friend, if it happens or if it has been happening; your response becomes very important. Remember: the **trap** is the momentum of going nowhere fast, and ending up with someone you never intended. This is, and can be the consequences that comes with impatience.

Please know: that if we fail to patiently enter- come out- or remain you could be tormented by these questions.

- What is wrong with me?
- What did I do wrong?
- Am I not good enough?
- What can I do to fix it?
- If I do this, will you then accept me/
- If I lose weight- cut my hair- not go to church etc….it will become self-abuse; if there is no self-awareness. PLEASE WATCH THE CONDEMNATION!

This list could go on because this is our impatient list; but also, our justification list of their mal treatment and rejection. We become so self-condemnatory without reflection that it may not be us at all. The sadness that goes with this condemnation, is your ability to conform to their abuse; and your fear of transforming your status quo. As long as you equip yourself with the inferiority; impatience magnifies itself within the complex.

Sometimes the rejection and denial takes such a toil, due to the energy we have put towards receiving affirmation from another. That's why going in with patience and assurance is essential. Not only patience and assurance, but also faith, with precaution. Be careful! **Impatience never looks for what is important.** In their arsenal; they go after your looks, your background, lack of ability, and even worse your religious beliefs. This is done to introduce you to their way of thinking. Rejection takes its form when your tolerance becomes high. It's their job to distract you from a new type of thinking. So it begins to counteract, your perceived notion that this is enough.

When you start to AWAKE: you realize you are better than their limitations. Please watch the trick. How we respond to the rejection will bring or destroy our sanity. People like to hold you to a level of insecurity in order to maintain supervision over your direction. It is the assumption of loneliness that creates this "Hurry up you".

I found out it is not what they say; it is what was fail to be said that sometimes have the greatest impact. Rejection is deliberate, but also it can be your deliverance. I would never been able to think, act and be the man that I am now, if I had never been rejected. **Remember: it is an unexpected opportunity.** Even though I didn't anticipate it, I can appreciate it. **Rejection sometimes is your release.** Don't allow it to stagnate you, allow it to elevate you. I have seen it cause isolation, also I have seen it cause over indulgence. I know it was emotionally painful. I know there was a pursuit for satisfaction and stability; but somehow, you found dissatisfaction and unstableness. **Remember: what seems to be a hindrance; if you can accepted it... has become your hurdle. Sometimes we find ourselves staying and lingering, because often it will signify defeat. Because we don't like defeat, we cling to what has rejected us from a warped perspective. This, if not monitored becomes our comfort, and convenience, and ultimately your controller. Tell yourself:**

- **I am not their limitations**
- **Their deliberate actions is my deliverance and activation**
- **I know how to blame myself/ but I also know how to forgive myself/ and celebrate myself.**

LEARNING HOW TO LOVE MYSELF!!!!! SAY IT-"I GOT TO LOVE ME"

My friend, if you fail to tap into the love that God has for you; then understanding how to love yourself will forever be a struggle. Is this a relationship or a relation trap?

Be careful!!!!

1. Low rates of prosaic behavior(lack spirit- dull in your imagination
2. High rates of aggressive and disruptive behavior
3. High rates of inattentive, immature, or impulsiveness
4. High rates of social anxiety

These will lurk after you until you allow it to sanction your demise. The reason it seems so successful with those who cannot wait; because of the senselessness that comes with your perception. So subjectively I impose these wide range of emotions, that want allow me to break the ranks of: stability- sanity- or satisfactory.

Look what it causes:
- **Frustration**
- **Intense anger**
- **Despair**
- **Even resignation**

This is not the time to shut down. However, for those who have felt the sting of rejection, its time rebound. I know through your sensitivity; you rather avoid controversy, reluctant to make demands, don't want to face the negativity, and have grown to rely on certain tolerances just to avoid potential rejections.

84

I have an announcement to make!
Whether you going in!
Whether you coming out!
Whether you are staying in!
It is time for the real you to come forth. Not timid (shy) - not tumultuous (confused-unrestrained) but the timely you. This you says "I got myself together". It says that yesterday was strong; but yesterday is gone, and today and your tomorrow you must own.

See, when we look for the acceptance from those who we didn't properly examine, then what is showing on the outside, is just a result of what we have internalize. The problem is that it now may be in a repetitive cycle. Impatient people often are infected by repetition. **It** literally seems like the same people, different bodies. It's almost as we cannot shake that spirit. Well, in essence you can't. What do you mean? Until you change your attitude, that same type of attitude you will attract. Yes, different body same spirit. You cannot continue to entertain with fragments, and expect a full / healthy relationship.

Be careful! That rejection doesn't become an expectancy. If it does, then every friendship-partnership- and most definitely potential relationship will suffer the onslaught of assumption.

The reason I had failed relationships after my divorce; I tried to run the relationship off of a reserve tank. I thought if I could entertain with the fragments, then I would be okay. Even though I was hurt, I was in a hurry, to select another hurt. We can't invite people into our dysfunctional world; and look for stability.

Can I tell you this? Always stay prepared to love, but always stay prepared for the "just in case clause." What is that?

- Just in case they flip
- Just in case they trip

85

- Just in case they decide to dip

You prepare your mind- body- and soul for the best, but never navigate or negotiate your sanity, just in case the worse shows up. **Your worry may control your hurry! Do not let this happen...**

Please know these things about rejection:

1. **Rejection is not your hindrance, it is your hurdle, it's a matter of perspective**
2. **Recognition of the positive you, comes with not accepting people's rejection of what you choose to change.**
3. **The extent of their rejection, usually comes from the intensity of your impatience**
4. **Unexpected rejection will open up opportunities. Do not reject yourself**
5. **Pay attention to your patterns- rejection may cause you to hide or camouflage true feelings, and accept unknown facts**
6. **Rejection can and will lead to grief- denial- and – bargaining- depression- and even acceptance.**
7. **Rejection will promote self-blame. Do something else with yourself.**
8. **Rejection will prohibit self-improvement.**

My friend, <u>rejection carries with it the symptom of impatience- hinders the reality of choice- and constantly allows hurry up as a solution.</u> This only intensifies your relationship decisions even the more. So many times what we recognize, and what we receive are dominated by deception. We will begin to bargain within ourselves to the point of conclusion, and confidence based off no self-improvement. **BE CAREFUL!**

Until you face truth you will deny the lie. What is the lie? You need another relationship- or I am ok. Survey says negative.

QUESTION TIME:
1. WHY DO I BEHAVE LIKE THIS?
2. HOW HAS OR IS THIS RELATIONSHIP IMPACTING MY OR OUR OVERALL HEALTH?
3. ARE YOU GETTING WHAT YOU NEED OUT OF THIS RELATIONSHP? IF NO WHY
4. HOW CAN I OPERATE WITH A DIFFERENT MINDSET THAN MY: PAST- PRESENT- FUTURE?
5. DO I OR HAVE I EFFECTIVELY COMMUNICATED WHAT IS NECESSARY FOR THE SURVIVAL?
6. DO I LISTEN OR CONTROL EVERY SITUATION?

Take time and answer:

This is your journal page for your answers. Be true to yourself.
   1.

   2.

   3.

4.

5.

6.

The most important thing right here; is that you **do not die from desperation**. Do not distant yourself from your destiny. I told you: when you negotiate your sanity, you maybe securing your displeasure. **BE CAREFUL!!!** It is right here you may come across as needy. So in your pursuit, quest to find the healthy relationship; you encounter and embrace an unhealthy one. It is your insatiable appetite, which creates a disregard for stability. So many time as we look for approval, we accept the confirmation that comes with these our mental traps. In our need to justify our assumption and our neediness will then reveal our ignorance. I found out, that your rejections are often triggered by the assumption. I told you in our ignorance of the relation trap…the assumption is often attempted to be justified. Your assumptions are birthed out of impatience. The impatience leads you to believe the time is now, it's time to go, or I really need to stay. We will become confined in our assurance; that we will refuse to do the necessary assessment. My friend, with assumption comes: inaccuracy- ignorance- as well as insensitivity.

- Inaccuracy- lack of correctness or being exact

- Ignorance- lack of knowledge or understanding
- Insensitivity – lack of thought, selfish

You assume you are ready, but don't know, didn't quite understand what it takes, but you keep proving through your thoughtlessness and selfishness your anxiety. If not careful, you will evoke these thoughts on the relationship, and provoke your mate. Because of lack of assurance in self.

Healthy relationships, and individuals do not jump to conclusions without foundational truth. How many times have you, we failed to check the facts, ask right questions, get right answers, explore other perspectives before diving in, or burning out. It is in our dysfunctional routines that we perpetuate our outcomes.

Example:
- How many times have you believed it would not happen to you?
- How much time have you spent trying to read minds vs. getting clarity? Remember: if you don't have clarity…quit behaving like you have clearance
- How many times have you believed your way was the only way? This will make no room for consideration. You believe its ok. However the indifference causes the relationship an injustice.

Why do we keep making these assumptions?

1. It reduces my fears- if you and believe based on my system of thinking and processing; I may not have to face the reality that it may not be truth.

2. I use it to answer my why questions- we look for validation to our answers. The sadness is: that most of our answers, and assumptions doesn't bring credence to the relationship. So we create these beliefs. This why the relationship is failing, this is

why it is turning or has turned. This could be the furthest from truth, but assumption denies clarity.

3. We use them to disengage from communicating- if not careful your assumption will begin to fill the void of understanding. So many times we don't like to talk, so we just assume. This will fracture a relationship. The less I say, the more it gives me time to believe, but not accurately know.

How many relationships have been damaged – hurt- and expired early because of your assumption?
How many times have you been assaulted, insulted, and wrongfully accused because of assumption?

Assumption:
- It destroys
- It don't trust
- It don't try to understand
- It makes bad decisions- financial, emotional, relational, physical
- It starts unnecessary fights
- It picks the wrong person, and reject the right
- It hold grudges
- It doesn't forget
- It reacts without clarity
- It causes confusion
- It employs confusion
- It intensifies damage, destruction
- It denounces credibility, and assures unstableness, it heightens wrong, and never calms fear

My friend, because we don't maintain our patience we give life to our assumptions. You cannot have, and will not have a healthy and constructive relationship…under destructive assumptions.

Check list time: Do you think like this?

- They don't love me
- They prefer someone over me
- My partner says these things because they should
- I need to keep my partner at bay
- I am not enough- pretty enough- good enough- for my partner
- I can't talk to them(have you tried
- They need me to be everything
- If we have a problem, it means I did something wrong
- My partner love his/her work more than me
- I must do something to get something
- It's my job to make them happy, even if I am not
- We should be automatically happy
- If they have been abusive it's a sign that they love(modify)
- I know they love me… no worries
- If my partner cheats on me, it's a sign I am not doing something correct

Take time to ponder these. These are all destructive assumptions. While carrying inaccuracy, they can make you feel inadequate. Learning to wait gives opportunity for renewal in your strength, and a rectification from your discomfort. Don't become so confined by your unstableness that you fail in doing the necessary assessment. We have become so keen in solving immediate, but lethargic about problems that require a more intense effort. So impatiently we move into something new, with someone new while denying the fact…we haven't resolve the old. It is the old that takes up residence and occupy space, while restricting your stableness. I found out that the provocation that fights your effort, and cause you to suppress versus deal with it. This will prohibit, and prevent in measures of problem solving.

Thereby causing you embrace; what will eventually displace you.

Dr Crabb says (I paraphrase) *that our personal stubbornness tends to avoid looking deeper, and evaluate our contribution to the problem we now face.*

My friend, we find ourselves impatiently pursuing the problem from our perspective. However, it is not always collective, as much as it is an individual problem. We cannot handle our impatience from a surface mentality…it is deeper than that. Look in the root; this is where the truth lies. Your impatience is a problem… and possibly now an addiction. So their cheating- rejection-lack of attention-detachment is at best surface.

Your impatience is the real issue.

Don't lean to your own understanding just for brief satisfaction.

Challenge: no more securing reasoning that allow this to persist.

Answer this: Is this relationship strong enough to allow you to relax, and feel unthreatened by others and their opinion?

Can this one work?

I was in a hurry- felt pressure- needed to be love…so impatiently I started another relationship.

We have spent entirely too much time trying to make unproductive relationships work.

Be careful right here.

You can cause your life to go unexamined and questions go unanswered. Check the interpretation of your thoughts. They may disallow free rein to your imagination. One of my favorite scriptures: trust in the lord with all your heart and lean not to your own understanding (Proverbs3:5)

It's our impatience that intensify our impulses. This impulse instinctively creates a sense of happiness that may not be accurate. Our impatience often forfeits self-love. So we began to hunt for people who will do our job for us.

This permits and increases laziness; when it comes to ourselves.

Let me ask a question…

DO WE MAKE PEOPLE RESPONSIBLE FOR LOVING US…WITHOUT LOVING OURSELVES?

Too often they will fail us…but be given the chance and the right because of the conditions we place on our happiness. **We have become so use to conditions, that, we fail in unconditionally loving ourselves. While we keep falling for them, we keep failing ourselves.**

Be careful!!! You may be setting yourself up for personal failure; due to lack of self-fulfillment.

Challenge:

- Do not become needy that you become greedy(anything will do)
- Do not die from desperation that you create an addiction for artificial relationships and love
- Do not sabotage a good potential relationship because the lack of patience and committing
- Don't allow impatience to forsake boundaries. It will cause you not monitor or manage or even maintain competence and discretion
- Don't allow impatience to cause an intensified jealousy. Thereby causing a regression back to the lonely and depress stage
- Don't allow impatience to approve false love- you may only force future pain
- Don't allow impatience to become your remedy for recovery
- Don't allow your impatience to become a permanent emotion
- Don't allow impatience to pressure your pick- it will pick your pressure

Be sober and vigilant. **WHEN YOUR WAITING ABILITY IS LOW, THERE IS ALWAYS SOMEBODY DESIGN TO DISTRACT YOU, FROM SOMEBODY WHO HAS BEEN DESTINED FOR YOU.** The needy you; does not recognize this. The essence of an authentic relationship, will be hindered by an artificial relation trap. Remember: you are going nowhere fast. You will get use to substituting, because of availability. **They may be tempting but are they timely? Right here. How many times have you accepted was artificial (you knew it) because your anxiety stated "it's taking too long."** My friend your ocular lust (what you see) will determine your now and deny your wait. **THEY KNOW HOW TO LUST YOU. DO YOU KNOW HOW TO LOVE YOU?** Part of loving yourself; **IS SOMETIMES DENYING YOURSELF OF WHAT YOU BELIEVE YOU NEED NOW. ADMIT IT! THE dilemma in my life is because of what I refuse to wait on. ADMITTING TO YOUR FLAWS, IS COMMITING TO YOUR FUTURE. START IT! SAY IT! I must commit to my future...the whole premise behind letting the process take place; is that you do not interrupt it with your inability to wait. Remember: do not rush readiness... it will happen on time because it is time**

Did I run them away? – Or are they holding me up list?

- Overly possessive
- Too jealous
- Average treatment
- Stay miserable or keep them
- Too clingy
- Extended worry

Look closely!!!!!
Part of our disappointments is in most cases; we want people to recognize, what we want respect ourselves. However, they realize that we don't recognize. You deserve better, but do you desire it. **WRITE YOUR DESIRES-Check it time:**

- Is it too good to be true
- Does it cause you, or are they in constant outburst mode
- What is the normal language in the relationship-motivating- degrading- uplifting- demeaning
- Is it feminine vs. masculine base
- Insulting complimentary
- Are you frustrated(psychologically)
- Is constantly living in the past
- Where there abused prior to you- this could affect the harmony
- Do they or you always find fault and blame
- Do they abuse you religiously or you them
- Do they use moods to control the relationship
- Do they or do you try to control

TRACK YOUR STRESS!!!!
Remember: HURRY DON'T WAIT!
We must still ask the question: Relationship or Relation trap? See here is the **problem** I must reiterate: **what you desire, may not be their conviction; due to what they think you deserve.**
Be careful! That your needy don't ruin necessary.
Remember: **either you are ready; and it will be successful or you are not, and it will be stressful.**
My friend, delusion is dangerous. Your anxiety will have you pursing, and perplexed. Without patience your perception will cause you to sink, if you don't think.

In closing this chapter you just receive some rules that will help you remedy some your anxiety concerning your impatient and loneliness

Things to Remember:

- Watch out for short-term gratification- because that is what it will be
- Get some control on compulsivity
- Quit expecting and looking for perfection in what you know is dysfunctional that only causes multiple relation traps
- Look out for selfishness in you and them- this may cause you to forsake a good thing and accept anything
- Don't deny relationship problems- and challenges
- Stop recycling pain
- As long as you repeat it…it will mistreat you

Impatience only hurries you to hurt again. **Patience is a virtue but impatience creates another victim. If you choose not to wait…then prepare to carry a greater weight.**

It may be time to start thinking about what you been thinking about…

REFLECTION TIME

CHAPTER 3

DID I STAY TOO LATE LEAVE TOO SOON?

REFLECTION STAGE

In this chapter we take the time to think about what we have been thinking about. It's called the reflection stage. **Too many times it is not about the readiness of the relationship; it is the reflection of the individual.** My friend, more than often we set ourselves up to become numb to the reality, that we are not ready. The evidence of this reality often progresses in increments. Then the nakedness of truth, hits all of sudden. It was little by little you had what was needed to depart or stay. It is in your contemplation that you tend to stagger with your conclusion. It is right here we begin to bargain without re-evaluating our boundaries. I shared at the beginning of the book: that sometimes 2 min can be too late and 2 years can be too soon. Either we are so impatient and can't wait on the thrust of the relationship, or we have been so disassembled in life, that any sign of trouble we scatter and relocate only using the pieces we think we need for our next journey. Here is the issue with this: we keep leaving pieces (broken pieces) while looking for partial placement and not wholeness. **It's at best we enter, re-enter, stay, or leave and become conditioned to operating off our pieces. Be careful! We will find ourselves staying where we shouldn't and leaving where we belong. The problem: this becomes normal, while our wholeness is illusory. Reflection.** We allow ourselves to live under this personal scrutiny, and allow the disunity; then we penalize ourselves with the ever presence of pain and longing. There is something that will always links you to truth. You may not like or accept it...but it is truth. Should I stay or should I go?

Let me ask you some questions:

1. **How deep is your commitment to staying, where you know there is nothing healthy about it?**
2. **How deep is your commitment to leaving, when you haven't considered what could be hazardous about it?**
3. **Could I be entangling an energy that will interrupt, corrupt and disrupt my life?**

It is in your inability not to reflect that gives the impression permission to produce the same results. We become what I call **empty pretenders.** The relationship does not have a foundation or a real basis to it; so we pretend it's full of all the essentials needed for relational success. It's not until we understand the insufficiency about ourselves, that we gain revelation on how to stop promoting unrealistic sufficiency about our non-existing relationships. As you reflect you will begin to discover and uncover truth about staying and or departing.

Is staying essential, is leaving imperative?

What is in your gut (intuition) that discloses the truth to you? Are you in agreement?

If you don't trust your gut, what is on the inside of you; there will forever be a posture of indeciveness. Be careful! You may stay in a mindset that never discover, or recover your uniqueness and self-worth; or you will be prepared to leave what has accepted your flaws and errors and patiently embrace your idiosyncrasies.

Are you in agreement with your understanding?

Confusion will always disown reality and discredit its existence.

This is why reflection is so important. **Confusion causes you to forsake and forget the one who desires, and places emphasis on you; for the one who treats you the worst...but you love them the most.** Reflection

It is here in this place that we confine ourselves to imaginary relationships that only exist in our minds. **THINK ABOUT WHAT have YOU BEEN THINKING ABOUT?**

Stop...

Don't let unwillingness rule over you again...

Being in agreement is essential, and also healthy to recover your thoughts. Do not reject your recovery, because you refuse to reflect I know this may be redundant; but I ask you again

Are you in agreement with your understanding?

Confusion will always disown reality and discredit its existence.

This is why reflection is so important. Have your **Confusion caused you to forsake and forget the one who desires, and places emphasis on you? Is the one who**

treats you the worst... but you love them the most?
Reflection

It is here in this place that we confine ourselves to imaginary relationships that only exist in our minds. **THINK ABOUT WHAT YOU BEEN THINKING ABOUT!**
What brings you joy/ fear?
Have you really listen to yourself?
Do I stay or go is not about a reward...it is about a reflection. Do you trust what's on the inside? Or are you compelled to keep pretending on the outside? Reflection. It's not my duty to know. However, this is my question.
Do you trust you?
I have set around years and pondered this same question. Sometimes in being truthful to myself, and with myself, I discover that I didn't really know. This is why reflection becomes a vital part to any, and every move you make. Remember: if you fail to reflect...you may possibly find yourself repeating.

Let me ask you some questions. **What makes a person cling to an abuser and hurriedly flee from the faithfulness of love?**
What it is about a damage person that seemingly draws damage people? The only thing they help you with is to increase the damage.
Why do we allow people to violate our being, while we dismiss it as a casual flaw?
Remember: It is not what they put us through it is what we voluntary allowed. So many times the relationship takes a plunge, or we feel the need to leave, because we fail to heal what is broken...so we master practicing in pieces.

My friend, when you don't trust your intuition, there is voluntary frustration that comes with your reality. Why stay? Why go? Are we trapped by the ever-present thought of need vs. want? What is it that we think we have/ are we sure? REFLECTION.

Will we seem better if we stay or go? Will it increase our bitterness, or calm our fears?

Have we become immune to non-support and poor dedication for so long, that your acceptance ruins the belief or chance that it really can exist?

Have you become withdrawn from the idea of genuine love; that you settle as long as it indicates a relationship? **If not careful, the very intake will expedite discouragement, but fall short in reflection. Staying or leaving is not always about a movement as much as it is about a mindset.** Until we get control of how we think, and what we are thinking about, we possibly could be trapped either way. What do I mean? You can stay but your mind has left...theoretically you are already gone. Or you can leave, and you should have stayed; then you end up somewhere with someone you never intended going nowhere fast.

Remember; you are required to establish your boundaries not expand your bondage. Attachment does not always exemplify togetherness...sometimes it denotes thoughtlessness. Warning!!! **Do not become so inconsistent with your stableness that you practice consistency with stupidity.**

So Tim why do we stay? I told you we do not trust our intuition or we fear reality. Next, I believe we are controlled and confound by our attachments. We have a plethora of reasons why we stay. Where you are now, or have been has it been helpful/ harmful or hazardous? Reflection. The more you reject the reflection, the more you grow a sense of abandonment and insecurity. Thereby, leaving a possibility of carelessness, and cluelessness. The accumulation of neediness to secure the safety of this relationship, will often position you not to make wise decisions. So we create for everyone including ourselves an impression of a relationship...while the extending our personal hardships. The sadness is: we too often find a place of security in it. Ask yourself: **Do I try to make it work knowing it is in vain?**

We have such a tendency to attach ourselves to people, places, and things, which cause us to become less aware of our surrendered mind, desensitize to the trap. **If you are ignorantly insensitive, you can become unconsciously bound, never moving from this type of thinking.** So you stay.

Well Tim, I can't afford to leave. I don't want to break no one's heart. If I leave, I'm not for sure if I'll find something better. The list goes on. **So we motivate our misery, by mishandling our mind.**

The attachment can take you and lead you from your true self, while the fear of movement causes you to doubt your true self. Be careful right here. **You will deny what has been created for you, only to accept what is created around you. What is around you can then effect what goes on inside of you. Do not forfeit you benefits by staying in something that is not beneficial.** If it becomes about convenience, then failure becomes an option. Then you can become convince to stay in a place (mindset) that is not purposed for you...but prolong your departure.

Question:

- Does it add value?
- Are they supportive?
- Does the relationship display mutual edification (benefits)?
- Do they present truth?
- Are there preventive measures in place?

Remember: convenience does not mean connection. Trust what is going on inside of you. Negative may be a part, but should never be the plan.
God's word declares: I have come that you might have life and have it more abundantly (John 10:10). Don't look for everything to be great...while accepting that which is less filling. In essence it is not that they were not dependable enough, you were not aware enough of your own self-suffiency that has been transferred to you by God himself. He did not create your bondage...you chose it. Reflection.
Be careful, what you tell yourself, because you may fail to believe there is better for you.
I am not an advocate of divorce, separation, or dis-unity, in relationships, but I am not a fan of any type of bondage or abuse. **Remember: Do not desert your peace, by operating on just pieces. Make sure if you going to stay, you are staying for the right reasons and not leaving for the wrong. If you are leaving, do it for the right reasons, and not staying for the wrong. Reflection...**
We get caught up in the idea of having, or keeping the relationship that the idea overtakes us. So it is at this point that we disconnect from the reality, and stay united with a falsehood. You will hold yourself hostage from your liberation. **Part of loving yourself...is trusting you.** This

will individually advance you to the opportunity that encourages your release. Dr Sonya Friedman says: *"if you don't like where you are in life, there comes a point where we must give up the part that holds you back."*

Did you catch that! **Give up the part that holds you back.** Remember: if you don't… you will never be afforded the opportunity for advancement.

I have discovered that we have become so directionless when it comes to our relationship, and its status. There is such a demand on our gratification, that our indulgence mixed with sabotage diminishes any reflection. It is the illumination of God's word concerning our relationships, which faces personal elimination due our unstable world. It is in these toxic, unhealthy relations that becomes problematic; but preserved the most. The true purpose of self- reflection is to correct our mistaken thoughts and actions. Here is the problem: **we are aware, but spend no time on correction. It is called "Ignored awareness."**

When we refuse this correction, we strengthen the problem.

- We don't learn from our mistakes
- We fail to detach
- We decrease our clarification
- We disallow a divine intervention

This is not just for your discovery…it is for your development in the will of God. Remember: **God created beauty, not bondage.** The fulfillment that comes with reflection, can aid in emptying the negative unproductive, mind repeating, insecure, fearful thoughts/actions that keep you trapped. The bible declares: that God has given us everything pertaining to life and godliness (2 peter1: 3). **It is when we become dissatisfied with our development,**

that we intensify our delusion, and are ruled by our contemplations. Do I stay or Go? Failure to think plays a major role in what we produce, how we promote what we produce, and our proclivity to why we do it in the first place. As we are pre-dispose to truth, our inability to accept it causes our confinement. If not careful, we will become satisfied being in a dissatisfied position. **We tend to pre-condition ourselves to discredit our strength concerning our ability to be liberated. If you don't heal from the history of thinking like this; you will only generate more bad memories.**

Common Thinking:

- I will never find love again
- They will not want me with these kids
- Even though it is bad, it is better than being alone
- I believe it want be like this always

So I prepare myself to stay stuck, and precondition my unhappiness that only renders my unproductivity. **If not careful you will keep arriving to right thoughts, but battling with the wrong conclusion.** It is in this catastrophic thinking that our battles become even more intense. Staying in any type of abusive, non-supportive-discouraging relationship is not only disheartening, but also self-sabotaging. If you fail in giving yourself credit for discovering better, you will ultimately discourage your necessary movement. If you do not begin to manage your mind, you will find yourself accommodating more than you bargain for. **Reflection.**

If you are so bold in picking your pain, it means that you are in a position to accept it. **Part of not trusting your intuition... is ignoring it.**

105

Let's see:

- **Do you feel a certain way constantly?**
- **Do you feel more drained and less fulfilled?**

Is there the constant exertion of power?

What keeps you here?

Are you ready to take action?

Are you prepared to no longer denying it?

Who are your supporters?

Are you confident in what you deserve?

These are self- awareness questions, which calls for reflection. Your liberation can be, will be complicated if there is no self-awareness of who you are. It will become even more difficult if you solely depend on others to maintain it for you, who will eventually deny your very existence. If not careful you stay under these conditions. You will plead for approval, while lacking self-awareness. **It is the lack of self-awareness that begins to protect the detachment. The distrust in us will always search for approval over awareness. Challenge: you must recognize your blindness to their weakness/ faults.**

Part of our dilemmas is we rather camouflage, suppress as if this is an antidote for the truth.

EVALUATION TIME

- **What trait is being exhibited the most? Does it bring out the best or worst?**
- **Are your goals discouraged, and accomplishments disapproved?**
- **Constantly blamed for their disruptive behaviors**
- **Pressured without consent?**

- Feel led to defend what you know is wrong, disrespectful, and unruly?

Reflection Time...
Part of our staying too late is we become use to the abuse, and feel obligated to the abuser. This is when acceptance disapproves of detachment. Your acceptance level will intensify itself. It is often at this point where our contemplation begins, our wisdom ends. It is also called **"ignored awareness."** I know the truth. However, I will not allow it to set me free. **It is in our stubbornness that our refusal secures our dissatisfaction, and causes us to stay.** It is right here where we fail deliberately not exploring, or exposing truth. In case I did not warn you, sometimes your tradition that causes your condition. It becomes: what I fear...then who I fear. Because you don't see anything changing, you order yourself never to make any changes.

Challenge: Never stay where it is not secured, and never leave a place God has sanctioned. Make sure...
It is our confused thoughts that immobilizes our confidence, and causes us to surrender our actions. It is when these actions become rigid; we create unwanted, unhealthy habits that deter us from thinking about what we are thinking about. So we fail to reflect on what could be, and should be in a productive relationship, and become acquainted with the wreckage of it... but never change it. So we stay because we refuse to see ourselves better. We choose to leave, because we will not reconcile our differences, and rectify that very thing that keeps us bitter. **When we do not recover our thoughts...we will not reflect in on our actions.**

107

So we stay in a relationship that cannot and will not help develop us, and leave one that has been designed for us. It all happens because of the lack of reflection. The way to properly reflect; is not to allow anything to rule your conclusion without any research. Our thinking has become minimal at best, that we maximize our uncertainties. So we will progressively decide, while not processing any thoughts. Reflection.

My friend, do not become guilty of not trusting your intuition. Do not depend on feelings, while dis- owning the facts. We want to be people saviors (next chapter). This is not your role neither is it theirs. However, trying to do it could cause even more issues. It is right here where the violation of your being can, and will occur. Do not dismiss this as some casual flaw…it is deeper than that. **Once again it not what you have been through…it is what you volunteered for. Say it… I volunteered.**

What are the facts?
Facts: are things that go deeper than how they appear on the surface. (Not a feeling)
Deeper will always say not ready. While surface says try it, do it, stay in it or leave it. Your feelings will more that often discredit intuition, and attachment in order to anticipate the survival of the relationship. Be careful right here. It is in the faculties of our mind that we grow a disdain for truth. I told you do not forfeit a peace of mind, while you allow your mind to fall to pieces. **Remember: we settle for what is not suitable only situational.** This stage should exhibit sound thought and action, but if not practiced will prohibit these things. My friend, your permission to these patterns of thinking will create a

stubbornness that becomes ignorant to the revelation of where you should be, and where God wants you. **So we conform and confine ourselves to a discomfort that only signifies companionship but does not edify our relationship with God. Remember: he created beauty not bondage.**

Part of your remaining will numb your loneliness, and validates a fantasize future. Here is the truth: you know differently in your mind...you just don't do different in your actions.

Too many times our head and hearts do not match up. When this happens we will fall in love with the idea of being in a relationship without reflection or reality. See too often I've discovered with certain individuals; that in their mind the relationship is already in existence, before the experience happens. It can seem right, but can also promote your destruction. **Reflection.**

I found out we want our desire but no direction. Part of our reflection is gaining a positive direction. The bible says: if we delight our self in him, he will give us the desires of our heart (psalms37: 4). It also tells to seek him first and everything will be added to you (Matthew 6:33). Make sure what you feel, does not introduce to you an addiction that destroys your sensitivity to what God has for you. **You may have the feelings... but do you have the facts. Remember: A 2 min conversation too long can cause a lifetime of repercussions and unwanted misery.**

Because there is no evidence of departure from these thoughts, you are ruled by your fabrications on why you stay or leave. Somehow there is a demonic presence that aids in our insensitivity, and induces our decisions. This produces a bewilderment from the truth. **Warning!!! Do not underestimate the destructive power of doubt. It starts as a temporary insecurity that can potentially create a permanent insensitivity. It chews away at the fiber of your foundation, while undermining a strong belief.**

- **Acknowledge your doubt- do not expect to overcome it, if you refuse to acknowledge it- stealthy problem (it sneaks up on you)**
- **Analyze your doubt-what is the logic- the reasoning- question the validity of feelings, bring them within reach**
- **Identify the source- where did this come from? (Child hood, past relationship)**
- **Ask yourself; is this a pattern? Did I overcome it? Or have I been suppressing it?**
- **Design a "better me" plan- come back from self – abuse**
- **Anticipate change**
- **Action time**

If not your doubt could hold you in a place that is not planned for you...or have you to leave a place that God has purpose for you.

So many times part of our repression comes from how we have trained our emotions to feel the way that they do. This in return leaves us dangling with a decision that doesn't need our attachment, as much as it needs our undivided attention.

Look at these personal emotions:

1. **It is too painful/ difficult to deal with**
2. **I am a procrastinator when it comes to my feelings- deal with it later**
3. **Have I become defensive in all my responses, and speculations toward every situation?**
4. **Do I lack ambition or motivation?**
5. **Am I growing spiritually?**
6. **Do I come off as suspect when it comes to someone loving me?**

Take time to reflect right here...
Do not avoid or reverse what is obvious, just because you feel, and is suffering from the obligation.

I stated earlier in the intro: that some relationships have no business in operation. However, due to the anxiety, and loneliness we frustrate ourselves, and gravitate towards it...even if it is abusive. It simply becomes a mandatory existence in our lives. This oblivious mindset keeps us in a place, with someone who does not comprehend our retention plan. If not careful the incomprehensive mind, can offset your sensitivity, and perplex the future of the relationship even greater. If you do not practice with caution, you may be overwhelmed by cluelessness. Here is the sadness: we create an expectation on others and a relationship without redefining ourselves, or reflecting on these things. This is why trusting your gut, and recognizing your attachments becomes vital. It will essentially help you understand your strengths and vulnerabilities in a relationship. Sometimes our attachments are established early, but become a model for our adult relationships. The sadness: it can determine the progression or the regression

of our relationships. This is our **style attachment**. However, the **model attachment** influences how each of us reacts to our needs, and how we are willing to get them met. The **secure attachment**, have you so confident, and self- possessed, thinking you are able to interact with others meeting both needs (yours& theirs). When there is an **anxious or avoidant attachment** you will select a person who inadequately (poorly & weakly) adapts to you. We may even select someone who isn't an ideal choice, but willing to make them happy. **Reflection time. Your commitment and attachment level has an uncanny way of distorting your future.**
Let's see:

- **I was shape this way early as a child, and I base the duration of my relations off this style only**
- **I am confident that who I am suffices for the both of us. – Secure**
- **I will go at any length to get it like I want it. As long as it stays like this the relationship can survive- Anxious/ preoccupied**
- **As long as I feel good, it's better than being by myself; I don't need my benefits to disappear, if they leave. Commitment**
- **Even though my emotions go voided, and needs become dismissive I believe in longevity. – Secure**
- **I am fearful you might leave me, I don't do well with rejection- Pre –occupied**
- **I will do it all for myself- I don't have to deal with no one- Avoidant**

I came across an article that stated: *"it is not the degree of closeness or distance that determines if the relationship will last, but whether do both partners like the same degree of closeness or distance. "*

What is the perception of your own happiness?

I told you; I am not an advocate of breakup, divorce, separation, but definitely not a cheerleader of bondage. We have to spend time on reflection. **Remember: when we don't recover our thoughts, we want have a remedy for our actions.**

Let me as some questions:

1. What has shaped your world early in life, which determines the only way you govern yourself and your relationships in your adult life?

2. Have you become so self-sufficient that you fail to hold others accountable for the responsibility to you in the relationship? Thereby making you the performer and the provider.

3. Do you position your mind to encourage the psychological harm that has been presented, just to get what it is you believe you must have? Why?

4. Have you become committed to not responding to abuse? Why?

5. Have you position yourself to stay in a non-reciprocal relation because of longevity? Why?

6. Have rejection daunted you so long, that you have become so pre-occupied with the thought of loneliness, that any attempt sends you in a state of distress? What rejection was it?

7. Have been so isolated that any attempt to show you mutual love frustrates your autonomy? You have become confident in not needing anyone to show you love- what cause the isolation?

Take time and answer these questions:

1.

2.

3.

4.

5.

6.

7.

Be true to yourself. Whatever the case is…truth shall set you free.

You may be:

- **Secure** –believe in others, can form close relationships
- **Preoccupied-** have only a sense of self-worth that depends on others approval and acceptance
- **Dismissing-** overt positive self- view- dismiss the importance of close relationships, denies distress
- **Fearful-** has a negative self-view, lack trust in others, subsequent apprehension about closeness.

If you fail to get to know them you will ultimately follow them. If you fail to know yourself then you may ultimately be stuck. Remember it is not always about a place, as much as it is about a mindset. Reflection.

Challenge: Do not ever feel unsure about your partner or unsafe about the relationship.

Do not feel the need to become clingy or possessive in order for the survival of the relationship. The relationship should never present/ require this type of pressure

My friend, it is in our failure to be true to ourselves that we search for personal justification as a means to our deliberation for freedom. Never acquiring the true essentials necessary to combat any ignorance that increase our disengagement from truth. Too many times we get caught licking our wounds, and it is here they we forget to manufacture our healing. **Be careful not to sacrifice your moment for a minute.** You get can become habitual in appeasing lust by leaving. Be anxious for nothing, but in everything in prayer and supplication, making your request known (Philippians 4:6). **Big mama help us: The grass is**

116

not always greener on the other side. Try not to stay confined in a place going nowhere, nor become over confident in going somewhere you not sure. Whatever you do just know, after you reflect. Too many open emotions extend too many opportunities. **It is not that we put our guards down we put our God down.** This is why it comes in like a flood, causing us to forsake our standards. Confucius tells us: one of the first ways to learn wisdom is reflection. With this refection your thinking becomes strong and your action become stronger.

Please consider:
- **Are they always jealous**
- **Controlling**
- **Put unrealistic expectations on you**
- **Trying to isolate you**
- **Blame you for their mishaps**
- **Over sensitive**
- **Forceful in sex to the point of abusive**
- **Batters**
- **Threats and violence**
- **Never see anything good in you**
- **Cruel to your child/ children**
- **Staying may not be your solution…**

Please consider:
- **Do they love unconditionally**
- **Do they provide unselfishly**
- **Do they except your weaknesses undeniably**
- **Do they motivate you unceasingly**
- **Do they listen understandably**
- **Do they know you unmistakably**

117

- Do they refuse to put you through any abuse unquestionably
- Do they desire to spend their life/ time unlimitedly
- Do they have a disdain for things that are ungodly

You should never consider leaving...

Part of a reflecting is:
1. Knowing your view
2. Collecting right thoughts
3. What to say, when to say it, how to say it
4. Develop and determine the right action
5. Management of time/ morals of time
6. How much effort to put in
7. Knowing the location of your mind
8. Where is my concentration/ do not violate your meditation-

Do I stay because I need it to work?

        Or

Do I leave because I don't anticipate it working?

Reflection only knows...

Let's change our perspective, and break some habits...

CHAPTER 4

THE MODIFYING STAGE

CHANGING MY PERSPECTIVE WHILE BREAKING
MY HABIT PHASE!

This is the stage where I must come to the realization, and
to the conclusion, everything doesn't need changing...but
something does. This is not about the people who you felt
did you wrong, because you impatiently selected them.
This is not about what they did, or said. This is not about
how many times they did it, and you allowed it. However,
it is about a thing called "accountability"...self-
accountability.
**If there is no self-accountability there will inevitably be
self -abuse.**
Please understand: **we must modify these dilemmas,
before we multiply our dysfunctions.**
Without making ourselves responsible, we ultimately create
a dependency on someone else to do it for us.
What partial changes or total changes do you need to
make?

This comes from a haunted past, or even something dwelling in your present, which can torments you even now. What could it be in your current situation that is good, but could be better if you made the necessary changes? Could it be that past has injured you long enough? Sometimes our past lingers, because of the permission extended to stay around.

I have learned that we have become masters of blame. Thereby, always disclosing what they have done, or doing, but never admitting to how I have mistreated/ and mishandled self.

Blame only holds them responsible...but never you accountable.

What changes are needed? Modify

I remember: starting to write this book, and reflecting by way of history the pain- problems- predictions- and even the predicaments that not others, but I put myself in. I became a master performer for every relationship. So I allowed people to identify me by my function, rather than appreciate me as a unique person. It seemed relationship ready, but in reality it was a relation trap. So I valued the perception and ignored the actuality. My friend, and because I allowed it (accountability right here) I created and gave birth to these perceptions. Don't fool yourself; when they have the function...they really don't need, nor do they respect the person.

Be careful! That you don't prioritize the function over personhood. "Staying too late or leaving too soon" was birthed out of: personal passion, pain and practice.

Did you know? You can become so pre-occupied with the idea of collective bargaining that your individual

boundaries can become altered-abused- and even abandoned.

As I picked up the pen to write, I had one goal in mind. To rebuild, revive, and redefine our perspective. It all starts with change. **However, with every change comes a challenge. If you can tell yourself (I can) face the challenge... you can forecast a change. Don't forget to thank God for the chance!!!**

As I look back, I now realize the environment that I grew up in, became familiar with, and admittedly loved, gave birth to this identity, and perception. Yes family, friends, neighborhood, and church all played a role in my dysfunction.

Because I didn't combat it intellectually, I embraced it ignorantly. I became what I saw, learned and yes even loved. (Pause) Is this you?

Behaviors are learned behaviors...until they become loved bondages. (Don't ignore this)

I remember: observing what I now know as abuse. I passed it of as an attribute to those dysfunctional relationships. So you see: what I considered normal, really was dysfunctional. I saw disrespect to women and from women. I saw dishonor for the man and from the man.

Look at the dysfunctional list:

- Cheating/lying
- Insensitivity/ manipulation
- Physical abuse
- Financial abuse
- Religious abuse
- Sexual abuse

These were normal cycles that became normal patterns, in which became normal perceptions. Now my obscured view of a relationship, was only defined by the intensified dysfunctions that I experienced, and embraced, also applied.

Remember: blame becomes available as long as accountability is not.

If not careful (like I did) you will become numb to these detriments. You will become comfortable being uncomfortable. When this happens: **you may deny the diagnosis in order to retain the thought that you have a sincere relationship. It's a trap. Modify**

Remember: they can become loved bondages. You look, you like you love, and they linger. They like myself loved and loved hard only to deny the diagnosis. Here was the problem: I didn't love myself. This will always be evident by your tolerances.

You will always either validate it (confirm it) and or satisfy it (please it). Because you believe that this is it; you become unified with the bondage. In most cases the bond is hard to break. Why? Because even though it is ignorance… it is agreement. What do I mean? If they have agreed to mistreat you, and you have agree/accept the mistreatment due to blindness then it's hard to show you any different. I recall so many times when the "I gotta have it" dominated the "must wait" attitude. See my friend, when we fail to acknowledge facts, and analyze truth… we fail, and we fall. Two facts about truth:

1. Sets you free
2. It can hurt

However, both are a cure for relationship blindness. Denial to these behaviors is dangerous. I was hurting so bad but denying it. While having all the signs, I still was ignoring the evidence. **Remember: there are always warning signs**

122

before failure. If you ignore them, then you can ignite them.

I realize now; I helped confirm their ignorance by showing my own. **Ignorance can and will help set you up for chaos.** My friend, if you fail to identify, then we will help intensify the illusion. **Remember fantasy does not mean future.**

Illusion:

- It seems different from what it really is
- Something that is false, but seems to be true
- The state of being intellectually deceived
- A pattern capable of reversible perspective

All this was a part of my life. I wanted to call it a relationship, wanted to believe it was the best thing I had ever experienced. The reality is: it fed my dysfunction, and I enjoyed the consumption. She was fine, it was so real, and definite. Here is the problem: I had said it with her, and before her, I said it. Sometimes, it can become so believable to you; that the reality will be revisited, and resisted by denial. It had enough power to reverse my perspective, and intellectually deceive me. Oh yes! She had the body, the beauty, but also she carried with her my bondage. The convenience I accepted in knowing was not the failure I had anticipated. I never saw it coming.

Delusions – a persistent psychotic belief regarding objects, self, persons outside the self that is maintained despite indisputable evidence that is contrary. It is believed to be true but actually false.

What have you accepted as truth? (Pause)- answer yourself

Too many times- same people+ same spirit= evidence-disbelief=results

The highest form of mistreatment is how you mistreat yourself. When you refuse to believe the dysfunction, and mistreatment, you perpetuate the deception. **Stop! Say it...** **as long as I refuse to believe the obvious, I will perpetuate my deception, and maintain my dysfunction.** So many times without analyzing the function we tend to continue in spite of indisputable facts. Like myself; we don't allow the evidence to introduce us to our consequences.

Be careful! **We will reject and neglect truth. Now what was prepared for us in the initial revelation...has been depleted due to ignorance and denial.**

I saw it, I felt it, but I denied it.

Until we transform our mind: we will not transform our matters. Your matters grow as your mind weakens. The truth is: when you don't transform, you will conform, leaving your condition deformed. But the question is...ARE YOU READY TO REFORM?

I failed to do a **function analysis**. My friend, because I failed to do so, it resulted in bondage. What is that? It is when you assess the connection between the behavior and the consequences. Simply, why do I keep doing this, and why does that keep happening? Part of our accountability is taking self- inventory. Part of changing your perspective, modifying, and breaking habits… is analyzing the function. It time to analyze:

• **Why am I functioning this way? Why am I accepting these terms?** Define for yourself and to yourself at this point. You must use specifications to rectify and not justify the necessary answers. If not, you will continue to condone and promote what is causing your relational demise. If we really pay attention: provided information is available that help render us from reaping unhealthy returns and realities. Did you catch that! THEY PROVIDE AVAILABLE INFORMATION- PAY ATTENTION!!! REMEMBER: DENIAL IS DANGEROUS. What happens: we become irresponsive to self –abuse, and when they expose theirs, we fail to recognize it, because we have convinced ourselves otherwise. I am sorry. This is not love, neither is it a relationship... it is becoming bondage. So the reality that exudes from their character, and intrudes on yours is revealed but rarely recognize. It is our denial and rejection that prolongs needful truth to aid us in our modification. What has been provided for you, that you choose to prolong because of the love for the bondage? My friend, the truth is: you are, as I was hunting for a healthy relationship while cultivating a falsehood. In one article I was reading; it says, without knowing what specific problem behaviors are, you cannot identify the solutions. Be careful! That you do not discard the severity of the problem for an unseen fantasy that does not exist...just persists in your mind. **Modify**. Some behaviors are not just by consequences. They are things that happen prior to the behavior. It is those preceding things that have a greater affect. Yes, it may create a behavior, but it may not always be the cause. Remember: your environment teaches you, and we are conditioned by what we learn.

• **What have I learned?** We learn them (**behaviors**) - we lust them (**consequences**)-we love them (**bondages**)- then they are lingering and lasting (**memories**). The book of James says: a person is tempted when he/she is dragged away by his or her own lust and enticed. My friend, it is your desire that pulls you into this type of behavior and has the capacity to keep you in this state of mind. It can become very destructive...but always delusional. It is the cognition (your mental activity) that we somehow create these delusional acts, which we find ourselves entertaining. It is when our minds stop processing this foolishness...we began to ask the necessary questions. Here is the sadness: we attempt to apply logic to our actions and reactions. **Are you learning? Or do you retain these conclusions that only, and have always encourage your distress.** In my study I found out: that we generate so many beliefs and behaviors regarding our ability to make these attitudes concerning our relations work for us. When we perceive that they are not working, then our perplexity intensifies, and our cluelessness begins. This is when the survival of our perceived relationships may be in trouble. **Let's pray. Lord help me with my thinking!** Very rare do we use the principles of learning and cognition to understand, or even change our realities.

Why? Because of the accountability that comes with and from effort.

Stop! Let's re-focus.

1. How do you define your status quo? Am I progressing from this type of behavior?
2. Are you able to measure this behavior?
3. Can I assess the very thing I have been covering up, but acting out emotionally?

At this point you either decrease or increase your behavior according to your personal belief.

Remember: I became my dysfunction. So I was suffering from a term called "**behavior deficit.**" It's <u>when you don't apply the appropriate behavior often enough- well enough-long enough-and strong enough.</u> Wow! Because I didn't apply the appropriate behavior to the situation I supplied enough ammunition to keep me bound to multiple relation traps. **Even though we choose our consequences... when do we change them? We too often repeat our rejections, due to our wanted desires.** Here is the problem: what we perceived to be mistakes are really camouflaged habits. **Remember: mistakes are made and habits are formed.** Literally: I keep on doing what I started, because something disallows the stoppage. The bible says: when I would do good, evil is so readily present. I find myself loving what I hate. When you start it; if there is no willpower to quit...you will increase it. **Modify.**

Remember: everything may not need changing but something does. If we fail in the things that will help us determine our consequences, we will continue to commit and submit to prepared bondages. Now unlike behavior deficit the "**excess**" is when I keep performing the same behavior too frequent- too strong. **Stop and think!**

Name some behavior excess that you will admit:

Think about I love what I hate! **Remember: if you do not modify, you will multiply.** On one end you don't perform

127

and the other you perform too much. If you are going to change the consequences, you may need to alter the aspect of your environment.

What are the features of your environment?
Who dwells in them?
When are your most vulnerable times?
How does it make you feel?
Why does it make you feel like this?
What consequence does it leaves?
No focus on it…will produce more failure from it.
Say it!!! I must focus on my change. What is inwardly and coming outwardly must be modified. If I don't change, it want change.
My friend, this decision must be deliberate.

- Make this mandatory
- Recognize starting doesn't mean completion it means process.
- Who have you socially trusted or who has helped you mimic a culture that aids in your deficiency and exerts a strong influence that cause an override in the area of stability?
- Are you sufficient enough to survive in this state mind?
- Do I need help? Who is/ what is the right help?

In Buddhism they believe that people can liberate themselves from life's inevitable sufferings. My friend, we have to practice, mental and moral purification. I told you we choose our consequences; but I also ask: when do we change them? The bible talks about pulling down strongholds and casting down imaginations. Tim how can I do this?

1. Let's locate the problem- you or them
2. Acknowledge the crucial items that lure you away
3. Be determine to break the attachment
4. Be determine to discern your influencers and inhibitors

We are so intrigued by our selfish desire, that we ignorantly keep chasing what doesn't want to be captured. Do not fall into this behavior. You cannot be drawn away from wisdom to appease your lust. It has rendered you the same results. **When you refuse to refuse...the results do not change.**
There must be a committing to a solution, not confusion about the problem. If you are not definite, then you will remain delusional, and always discover another relation trap.
Do not look outward... this is an inward condition. **Remember: you have the power to liberate yourself.** In most cases the prerequisite to your behavior deficit and excess is that you abuse yourself. For me it wasn't hard since I had learned it. Even though it bothers me now, I watch people prioritize pain. When I became a recipient of it, I didn't combat it, I accepted it, because in my world it was also my reality. So many times our perspective is limited due to the extension of our pain. Because the fear of the diagnosis and what will occur, we will deny the existence of it. Be careful! **You may want a collective bond, but do you possess an individual identity.** I needed her to love me, while abandoning self-love. I was trying to make her responsible for my personal responsibility to myself. **Pause.**
How many times have you got caught in this trap?

Are you in it now? Will you ever own the reality and manage the remedy

How do you determine never to be there again? Modify.

Can I keep it real? I always deserted me, and trained them how to treat me, while I failed the course on loving myself.

Warning!!! While furnishing them with nourishment, you can become famished yourself.

Because I grew up in dysfunction, I was trained to call it a relationship. It was hurting me, but I gave it permission to hold me.

Stop! Gather your thoughts. What have you allowed to hurt, but hold you at the same time?

See my friend, if not careful we will train our minds to think like this, and tame our tongues from speaking against it. We come to conclusions and remain insensitive to our own pain. Remember: ignoring it ignites it. As I did: we allow the pain to grow and become emotionless to it. So the more it hurts, the more we love. It's called "self-abuse." Remember: what we are hurt by we hurt with. **Modify**

I found out when you are not taught the signs; then submission to them becomes a pattern, and creates a lifestyle. I was trained to settle. Oh boy did that hurt!

Looking back now: I placed too much trust in a perception, without my personal pursuit for truth. It was available, but denial made it undetectable. This couldn't be happening...in retrospective it was. **They don't always have to speak it to you, to show you...but you better speak it to yourself to acknowledge it.**

In public, I was the man, the hero, and everybody's boy. However, in private felt like the failure. It was hurting. But

I was holding on for dear life. Relationship or is it a Relation trap? **Remember: fantasies don't mean future.** Have you ever felt disrespected, devalued, and dishonored? But you still discredit the evidence to support the love. Even though you know the obvious, you still expect the same. Sadly, my delusional moments did not help a needful deliverance. This deliverance: was not about her it was about me, from me. See prior to this one... was another. You often give birth to either your illusions and or your ignorance. I was trapped by own self- imposed paralysis, and handed out permission for people to maintain my handicap. **Be careful! You can be tricked by fantasy and cause it to trap your future.**

Don't fall for these traps:
T-ricks
R-eady
A-pplying
P-ain
S-low

- Is it time for change?
  1. What do I change? Why that?
  2. Will it affect what I perceive?
  3. What patterns have you locked into that you call normal?
  4. Do you feel like you are trapped? Why?
  5. Are you confused between places?

These may need to be asked / answered to consider the necessary modification. If you don't take time to modify, you may take on the illusion of perfection within your relationship. Thereby, discounting the fact that the polar opposite exists. Do not forget to remain true to thy self. Introspection is needed. Failure to monitor your changes,

131

and manage your changes, will result in you becoming even more distant from the truth. Have you trained yourself to ignore rejection just to caress it with passion? Remember: it can be beautiful, have a nice body, but also hold your bondage. I found out the more I desired to get away, the more I was drawn to it. When I thought I had a mastered plan, she had already mastered the play. I had surrendered my vision, only to succumb to her victimization. I hated and love it at the same time. **Be careful! It is when you try to break away; your suspense want let go.**

If you don't start the modification process you will comply with a self-help program designed to have you with someone you never intended, going somewhere you never desired. Relationship or is it a relation trap?

Most of our chances/changes are normally hindered by our traditions. It is these patterns that will always fight and frustrate progress. Until we make the necessary changes, we will hold up some wonderful chances. **Modify**

How long will this contemplation last?

- Do I base decisions off of past experiences?
- Do I know what I want/need?
- Have I allowed selfish people to dictate, determine and define my outcome?
- Do I bring credence to others misinterpretation/
- How long will I penalize myself, my destiny by not processing my pain?
- Do I even believe I am an opportunity, not someone's option?
- Have my own traditional views trapped me?
- Do linger in my disappointments and still remain delusional in my decisions?
- Have I remained so non-responsive to deliberate hurt in order to maintain a relationship?

If not careful we will take on a frivolous (playful) nature about what should be serious. This is done in order to disengage from either rectifying it, or rectifying us.

My friend, part of changing our perspective is to target our frustration. Ask yourself: how has your values-expectations-history- and experiences-been able to filter thru. One of the main reason we lack in identification, is we lack in skill management control. Remember: **we learn these behaviors and lust the consequences, and love our bondages.** Because this has not been identified, it never gets rectified. Why? We do not exercise restraint. Thereby, leaving us with lingering memories. This can be detrimental.

1. We don't resist temptation
2. We do not exercise restraint over impulses, our emotions, and even our decisions.

This will leave us gratifying in the moment, but grimacing over the memory.

It is right here; that we attempt to manipulate people's interpretation. We for so long have tried to get people to understand, that in which we can't explain to ourselves. The failed expectations, the relational history, and experiences should have cause a decrease in my behavioral performance. Due to the fact that I perceived this was a part of loving me; I increased my more destructive behavior.

Modify

Here is the problem:

Habitual behaviors will always have habitual consequences.

In the bible proverbs 25:28 says- *a man that cannot rule his spirit is like a city without walls.*

Remember this: No rule-No restrictions- No restraint-No results- No relationships

Do not be confined by this penalty of thought. However, confirm the adherence by modification. So many times I was conformed by the words of deception, that I was not confound by wisdom. It is in our allowance that we will give access to that, which cannot aid our solutions. We have this uncanny way of mimicking certain behaviors, and mastering the bondages that comes with them. This will cause an over indulgence, leading us to forsake regulations and losing self-control. **Remember: no rule, no relationship.**

What has been the thing that has caused you to forsake regulations and lose all restraint?

Write it down right here. _____

Remember: the truth shall set you free

Mine was sex and more sex. As long as the presence of sex was available, the absence of love didn't matter. To tell the truth it was what I wanted that created a dismal view of what I needed. My definition of relationship was sex/perversion. It also became my lust, and my bondage. **What we are driven by, we also can drown in. Remember: the original intentions, may not always keep their undivided attention**. When the relationship needs more than what we originally designed for and by; the termination is sure. I found out; if we live by it we possibly die by it. I based it off a feeling and not a fact. While I was creating a feeling, I was dissipating my future. **You cannot build it on feelings…you build it on facts. Pause.**

Please, do not become so use to this type of behavior from them or to yourself that you abandon your worth. Do not allow this to become acceptable (I did). Can I help? **If you**

posture yourself to accept this; you help position them to expect this. You can become so busy trying to feel good that you become numb, and have a disregard for self-abuse. **If there is no emphasis on your uniqueness, there will always be an expectation of your weakness. Modify.**

My friend this is why the analyzing of your function is vital. What I see, feel, perceive, what purpose does the behavior behind it serve? How can you make stronger/reassure the reinforcement of what you know is necessary for the fulfillment of the relationship? Your expectancy of them, without the reassurance of yourself; does not always secure the reinforcement needed for relational solutions. If not careful we will exert a lot of energy on manipulation of them, without introspection of ourselves. Be careful of mental masturbation. This is a process that only satisfies you and your thoughts. It is where you engage in intellectual stimulation, and conversation with little or no practical purpose. Literally, you get off on satisfying yourself mentally. Did you catch that? While emotional stimulation, you extract from yourself at the same time. It is pleasurable but unproductive. **Modify**

I found out: it is not that we don't want to change. However, the problem is doing anything differently, or thinking different either ceases or the degree of difficulty kills the effort. Psychology today had an article that blew me away. *It stated: that in your mind what you believe to be true; is either true or becomes true within a certain limit.* **Remember: perception without truth is just perception.** If we lack strategies designed to correct behaviors, then we prepare to remain the same, and reap the same results. Stop and think:

- What has been imposed on me that I continually entertain?
- Why do I leave no room for alternative perspectives
- How much power have I given away?
- What have I overtly and covertly been instructed to avoid?
- How many times I said yes, when I knew it was a definite no?
- Why do I continue what should have been stopped?
- Am I able to stop it?
- What is my orientation (where do I go)? Where have I been?
- Do I have any control?
- What needs to be eliminated?
- What do I have to assimilate? (adjust)
- What are my other possibilities?

Take time to answer each one of these. To thine ownself be true.

1.

2.

3.

4.

5.

6.

7.

8.

9.

10.

12.

I hope you were truthful to yourself. There has to be some positive replacements to our habitual behaviors, and old patterns. If not it will be evident in every type of relationship you try to build. Whether romantic or platonic, if there is no rule, there is no relationship. Do you have a clue when this behavior comes in existence, and how you carry it out? **If not careful the existence of it will meet your resistance to it. Modify**

If we are to begin locating a resolve we can no longer deny the fact that it exist, and the fact I have been resisting the truth. Remember: blame doesn't hold you accountable. This is not about them; this is about the exposure of some habitual behaviors, denying you the fullness and the production to have happy, and healthy relationships. **Say it...I will not deny the exposure I need any longer. Let's pray.**

Dear lord, expose everything I need to know about me. Create in me a clean heart and renew in me a right spirit. Perfect those things concerning me. Lead me not into temptation and deliver me from all evil. If you find anything in me that hold up my progress reveal it to me, and give me the strength to recognize it, and remedy it. I desire better, bigger, and a brighter future. Amen

My friend, <u>**your exposure of it, starts your closure to it.**</u> So many times we will resist aid because we carry the arrogance of a flawless relationship. This relationship will lack nourishment and starve from growth. If you train yourself to exclude the exposure of negative, and unproductive behavior you could be doing the relationship and injustice. Relationship that starves from growth, most times are those that resist needed exposure, and risk losing restoration. **Modify**

Have you ever recognize the one thing that requires reflecting upon the most, we most often resist?

The reason we become numb to our discomfort...is we fear change

In my book Unstable I state "that **the biggest enemy you will ever have to fight is the one you pretend that is not there."**

What is it that you know, but has convinced, and have conveniently supported your resistance?

Be careful that you don't continue on the road of hope, without a reality check, and truth. Effort often can meet resistance, based off your level of fear to make some necessary changes. When you accept their terms and surrender yours. The modification that was accessible now becomes, and is subjugated by those who recognize your dilemma. **Remember: to modify these dilemmas before we multiply our dysfunctions.**

Be careful right here…self-abuse is an inevitable if no self-accountability. Your personal criticism, coupled with their intimidation, and manipulation can easily become your stronghold. When your modification starts, then the elimination of certain behaviors will cause them to cease.

Answer these:

- Do you trust your perception? Ans. If no then why?

- Do your mind constantly berate (criticize) you with negative overtones?

- Do you battle/ blame yourself because of their behavior towards you?
- Do you constantly give people access to re-open your scars allowing the injury to deepen?

Not recognizing and responding to the need and care of change may cause you to identify, but never rectify. Dr. Crab says, *"Most of us are not good at observing ourselves and reflecting honestly on what we see."* This is correct.

Because we do not practice self- accountability, we will at some point perfect self- sabotage. In my gratitude, I thanked the lord for opening my eyes to my self – awareness and my self- worth.

You cannot refuse to see, neither refuse to say, that you are better than your pain. It is time for you to modify. Quit making yourself so obvious and oblivious because there is no mandate on you, to make yourself responsible.

Very rare do we want fix what's wrong, what is broken or even know what is wrong or broken. Why? There is a part of us that just don't want to deal with it. Personal repairing never seems imperative. This is due to the fact that we based every problem from a plurality issue and not from an individual perspective. **Remember: blame is only an excuse not to hold yourself accountable.**

We become:

- Aggressive- too
- direct, judgmental and undermining, we invalidate, become critical, analyze, belittle, demeaning and controlling
- Denying –we don't want to acknowledge reality- we refuse to listen- withdrawing, we think silent is beneficial.
- Minimizing- act as if things don't occur, we act as if it is not impacting us- we maximize their trust by minimizing our personal trust.

Hey if we don't fix this…we fail this! Say it… if I don't fix it…I fail it.

I became my dysfunction. **My friend, if your discipline doesn't show up your dysfunction will.** So many times we will forsake our sanity for a false security. Thereby, increasing the chance for the dysfunction to intensify. Because I minimized God's love and self-love I created a security through perversion and sex. This was the pre-requisite for every relationship I entered. It was decision based out of dysfunction. I used it as my satisfaction, and allowed them to use it as their manipulation. Be careful!!! I recall: going over to the houses on the street. There were many of the older women that would invite me over to do little task, and little pick up jobs. I know you say... there is nothing wrong with that. You are right in your assessment. It would be what I encountered while was there, that gave birth to my dysfunction and perversion. Everything from nudity, to sexual acts that distorted my perspective on what real relationships should be. I thought what they were doing, saying, and how I was feeling was okay. It amazes me how we allow our negatives to be our nurturing. It was that spirit (that attitude) that consumed my thoughts, and shaped my world.

It may not be your fault...it just may be your fight.

Your perversion can become your pleasure...and your pleasure become your punishment.

Remember: if we don't fix it...we will fail it.

How many battles have you lost within yourself; because of a refusal to fix what is obviously wrong? Some of our major decisions have to come from breaking the tie that binds to this attitude. See I didn't break away from sally before I got started with sue. The residue of the last still held weight. Due to lack of modifying, the pressure of the perversion was planning my next punishment. I didn't break or digest the binding tie, so I latched on to a familiar in order not to lose relationship status. Be careful!!! You must make sure that you are not still connected. Why? The residue, reflection, resemblance, of that relationship or trap can cause the reckless results...THE relationship, or you intended. At some point where you left off, will eventually manifest itself in another. You will find yourself in a very deficient (incomplete) posture. This disallows the fullness of you from coming forth. In return a part of you is offered;

141

due to the fact you don't trust releasing all of you. This is creating unhealthy relationships, and secures a relation trap. **Until you find a way to reclaim all of you…do not submit another part of you**. This will always affect your ability to receive and limits your capacity to get a total person, not just a function. **Remember: if discipline doesn't show up dysfunction will.**

So many times we will enter into these agreements with no sincerity, only to fall in love with our insecurities. Thereby, creating anticipation that leaves us deranged and confused. In case you did not know: **An unhealthy anticipation MORE THAN OFTEN becomes a painful termination.**

MODIFY

In the book on breaking soul ties the author states: that we create sentimental worth, but no sacred wisdom. He also states: these relationships are damaging and even demonic.

My friend, whether we know it or not; too often we tie ourselves to people who often help us re –connect with old patterns and disconnect from our newness. This is where your battle for rectification, liberation and even modification starts. Here was my dilemma: different body and person same spirit reconnection, never disconnecting from the old. So even when going the aisle, you can marry your dysfunction. What should be a Holy ceremony; can be diluted and a sentimentally delusional creation. **Modify**

This is why we cannot deny what is necessary for our revival and our reversal. This in itself will minimize our healing, while maximizing our pain. **It is our suppression…until it becomes our depression. My depression creates a dependency on my dysfunction.** With the gun stuck in my mouth, hand on the trigger, ready to take my life. My perversion was ready to punish me. My friend, when you don't value your life... you often will become a victim of it. I thought it was over when they were over. Remember: it is a lingering memory. It can become such a lingering thought that will introduce itself to every relationship, and every relationship expires the same way.

Modify

I found out: when you don't take time, to make time, to recognize wasted time...it is the wasted time that forsakes the time, to make the time for change.

The wrong memory will steal the right moment and movement.

It was due to the lack of recognition of who I was, that I repeated the reflection of the memory. **Modify**

If not careful what you begin to speak can become your burden.

- I'm never going to have a productive relationship
- I must not be good for anyone
- All the best ones are gone, so I just settle
- It just don't last
- Something is always wrong
- I can't do this no more/ want do it again

Your mouth precedes and produces your misery. Remember: trust in the Lord with all your heart, and lean not to your own understanding.

It was my negative self- belief, that became my negative self-talk, became my negative self-pity. This is when we muster up an ego problem. You know: I am good- I can handle this- it's no big deal- I will fix it. Never committing or admitting to yourself or others or even to God: I am scared- I am confused,-I am insecure- I can't handle- this is too much for me to handle. It is your isolation and your withdrawal from this present reality, which produces the greater stress. This fueled my loneliness, motivated by suicidal thoughts. **Remember: burden will neglect boundaries**

Can I help?

My understanding ruled out my GODLY KNOWLEDGE.

- That I am more than a conquer
- That I am above only
- That I can do all things through Christ
- That with his stripes I am healed
- That I can pull down those things that try to hold me strong
- That I can cast down imaginations
- That the joy of the lord is my strength
- That through him I don't have to fear anyone or anything

This is who you are. SAY IT!!! This is who I am.

If you will forget these things, you will forsake who you are. **You must learn to trust what is going on inside of you. Don't forget this: whether going in, coming out, or staying in. Often times the truth is closer than you realize. If not you will base your conclusions on who or what is on the outside. Make these be some daily declarations in your life. This is so they can remain as some future inspirations as needed.**

1. Recognize - what you can't afford, and what you are not willing to tolerate. What patterns have got me in this position before
2. Decisions come with clarity, and delusions stifle sanity
3. Rushing to remedy often rules over restrictions
4. Don't commit yourself for the wrong reason
5. Try focusing on the process rather the content
6. Do not be reluctant to change

Until you begin to make some of the necessary changes, you may be holding up some wonderful chances.

This is what modifying is all about. I make the necessary changes I need to make, when and how I need to make them. You and I must begin to decide is this a habit or a pattern. It is the habit that I find myself doing every day. The pattern compel you do it…even if you like it, but feel like you must have it. Be careful!!! THE Danger zone is ahead. The pattern makes you feel obligated even though all signs point to stop, do not enter, under construction closed for remodeling or unsafe. Your habit normally requires a certain pattern of behavior. **Stop! Ask yourself what changes are needed? Remember: your behavior will introduce you to your bondage.**

If personal transformation is going to take place the recognition of the pattern has to start…and the repetition of the pattern has to stop. A painful memory usually follows a permissible pattern.

If I will admit anything; I was stuck in a pattern. It held up my release, and my recovery due to incompetence. The bible says: a dog will return to his vomit. Well, I kept returning to the point I didn't even think about it. Because there was no elimination…I experience no transformation. **Say it! No elimination there will be no transformation. Challenge:**

- Take inventory of your repeats-
- What were the dominant emotions at the time?
- How many were failures? Define failures based off the situation

I found out in my personal assessment that familiar becomes comfortable, even if it means failure. There must be reinforcement of this undisciplined behavior. **Modify.**

If you don't repent you will repeat. This will allow everyone you come in contact with to take a piece of you, and allow you to give a piece of you away. This in return halts the process of wholeness. **Until getting yourself together becomes a priority, falling apart will take precedence.**

You cannot find, or will not find the love you need in conditional territory. What is that? It is the place and the people who require that particular function we talk about. That your performance only meets their requirements, standards, and comply within their needs, only satisfying theirs and disqualifying your value. Without restraint you will have a tendency to surrender to another trap. If you don't request help with your history, you will either hurt or repeat with your history.

Let's admit it right here: change is needed now. Remember: this is about you; so do not make this moment be about no one else.

1. You can no longer keep sacrificing your sanity for brief moments of satisfaction
2. You can no longer keep doing the same things looking for a different results- you will only attract the same.
3. You must find out what is strengthening you and what your weakness is. Are you getting stronger or weaker/
4. You must keep the knowledge center open. Be prepared to detect any intruders. Remember 2 min. might be too late.

146

5. You must always be able to identify barriers, problems, and defenses with self before notifying others. You must know that you are not ready...before you show others.

One writer stated: "what we call chaos is just patterns we have not recognized." Have you took time to decipher, what you choose to believe is just random. Please, do not take this behavior for a random act. You must learn the cues that will determine these type consequences that come with this behavior.

Warning!!!! Relapse

Remember: if we don't modify our detriments we will multiply our dysfunctions.

Relapse – a return to a former state, especially after apparent improvement

Do you even know that there is a problem calling for change in you? In some cases recovery, can pose a problem. Why? It begins pull on the new to discharge the old.

Challenge:

• **Evaluate honestly- is the relationship healthy or unhealthy? Have the relationship or I changed since the beginning? If yes. Why?**

Be careful of ignorance, and resentment that it doesn't hinder the maturation of the relationship or personal growth.

Be careful of volunteering one- sided commitment. It may just expose desperation

Be careful not to release too much information. It can lead the interpretation and intensify your frustration.

Be careful of self-implosion. Then is when you will collapse on the inside, while camouflaging on the outside. You never discover you uniqueness, but always

recovering from your weakness. Always asking the familiar question "what is wrong with me?"
Be careful of delusional pathologies
Please be true thyself.

All this is a part of modifying, but can increase what we call disorders. Things will never come together nor will we have success in our relationships until there is a conviction within self. If there is no attention to your convictions, you will continue to disregard instinct, and intuition. All evidence should guide you to a reality. However, despite what you know, what you see, and how you feel, you still embrace another relation trap. We become so settled by these fixed beliefs that our personal sabotage increases while improvement decreases. Be careful!

Don't be trapped by what you think you need or by what you think you already have.

When you don't prevent certain things, you will practice many things. When you keep practicing these things…something is bound to prevail over you.

Now, this pretense that is constantly presented will consistently help predict your predicaments. If there is no presiding over your emotions, feelings and even your decision making; then the precarious position you stay in, will always be a prelude to your extended misery.

Do not pre-occupy yourself with the idea…that you are alright. You are not. Modify. Part of changing your perspective, is prescribing to the essential things that will produce: emotional, mental, psychological and yes physical transformation.

Remember:

- **The more you struggle with change…the more attracted you become to the pattern**

- No prevention intensifies the tolerance
- Delusion will always deny weakness
- Your weakness unlocks the door to your unstableness
- Lack of awareness or adjustment could possibly lead to abandonment of your alternatives
- If modification is not your reality, than dysfunction will become your lifestyle
- Your relational maturation is contingent upon your ability to modify.

As we leave this chapter, take time to take introspection of you, and the necessary changes in your life that is needed. **It is the people who pretend they have it together, that usually scatter the pieces.**

If you are going in… check the changes

If you are coming out…check the changes

If you are staying, and looking for better…check the changes

5 rules to your modification:

1. Modification must mandate momentum
2. Modification must model maturity
3. Modification must maintain, and monitor a changed mind
4. Modification must motivate morality
5. Modification must minister a message

- I need change
- I am changing
- I have changed

Modify changes, do not multiply dysfunctions.

ARE YOU READY? LET'S SEE…

CHAPTER 5

ARE YOU READY STAGE?

MATURATION PHASE

Every successful relationship must have a strategic plan on how it will work, and remain working. **If there is no planning... there can be no partnering. If there is no partnering, it could interrupt any and all potential.** In every relationship there is the potential for disparity to rule. However, with a plan in place, and powerful partnership, that which is recurring and problematic, will yield due to the influence of oneness. Can I help? There is no relationship that is exempt from challenges, and even confusion. This often is due to what I call **selfish interpretation**. This is when I gain knowledge only from my understanding, and refuse to accept any other. Be careful right here.

Every relationship must begin with the denial of self... not the absence of self. This stage will once again calls for a comprehensive mindset. This is with the understanding: this is a shared experience. This is not about rescuing

151

someone. However, it is about reviving understanding, and returning to a godly design... that we should not be alone. There must be an appreciation for the individual, and the search of unity. The one who has been created to share in your weaknesses, as well as appreciate your uniqueness, has a great task. Most times we tend to fail in our efforts. Why? It's in our efforts, that the relationship calls for greater output, that surpasses our fatigued minds, and bodies. In this stage we cannot dominate with our selective perceptions, while failing to practice unification. There can be such a dominance and concentration on personal superiority in the relationship; that the maturity is rarely exposed or experienced. Remember: this is a shared experience, not just for individual exposure. **Are you ready for this?**

Part of the maturation phase is nurturing. Proper nurturing will always come from a progressive maturing. As your relationship progresses, there will be a need for discernment, discipline, and devotion on what type of nurturing is necessary, based on the level you are on. If you use this for a superior moment, based from an alleged inferiority, you may hurt the chances of a productive relationship. Part of our nurturing is:

- Accepting the fact that challenges will come. There will always be chances to channel through these challenges, and make needful changes
- Enduring the urge to flee at the sign of conflict
- Keep a prevention plan in place.
- Do not ignore easy fixes, leaving the opportunity for them to become wild fires
- Prioritize feelings, do not victimize according to your interpretations

- Learn the art of serving your mate. This is not from a slavery mentality. However, it is a sacrificial attitude.
- Work on, and allow your love to grow, becoming healthy for one another
- Learn each other's language.
- Be cautious of deal breakers. These are often selfish in their nature

Do not allow assumptions, to forsake judgment. This will only encourage your conclusions. If you are incorrect, it can and will only frustrate the direction of the relationship. The relationship may not need more intimacy and climatic ecstasy. It may need: **social integrity, emotional motivation, intensified confidence, unscripted security,** and most of all a **godly presence.** If this goes misunderstood, the destiny of this relationship could be detained, or terminated due to inaccuracy. **Be careful with the battle between clarity and assumption.**

Let me ask you some questions:
- What development is needed in this relationship?
- What development did you miss/ rejected in the last?
- Know the verbal, and the task needed
- How can your experience educate them, without demeaning them?
- How can you or do you assure the promotion of their thoughts, through encouragement/motivation without intimidation?
- Have you refused to nourish the one you have? Why?

ARE YOU READY FOR THIS?

Part of knowing your mate is learning them, and prescribing to their needs without capturing them, and controlling them with your wants. Too often this self –imposing behavior creates conditions that will only validate and supply for self. If the relationship is going to survive, and have strength it will come through maturing, and nurturing. **Do not suppress the painful parts of your relationship.** In doing so; you can hurt the chances for development. In this maturation stage you may discover the inconsistency in feelings, but also the opportunity to resolve it with **consistent validation**. A carnal rule of mine: **don't just recognize their weakness...without reviving their uniqueness. It may be a fact. However, it doesn't have to be the future.**
Are you ready for this?
Mutual nurturing is necessary for every relationship at some point. This is vital. Why? The relationship can grow one-sided. This is where only one is receiving, while the other is starving for development, and cultivation. **If we deny this fact, we possibly deny the relationship's future.** This question will begin to seem redundant...BUT are you ready for this? If there is a lack of understanding, the essence of the relationship may decrease in appreciation. If there be domination, it only signifies insensitivity, and insecurity. This is why making a sacrifice plays a major role. Why you may ask? In observation we tend to disregard the aggressiveness of our personal anxiety. However, in this stage we must acknowledge them, and make adjustments, while both parties pursue the well-being of the relationship. Making these adjustments takes on introspection and humility. This in return helps us to refute and relinquish our beliefs of a convinced dominance. If not careful, you will abuse your partner's

heart, by what is rambling off in your head. So many times when one or the other partner exposes their weakness, they are asking for help…not for embarrassment. If we fail right here; we become guilty of abusing the relationship. This is called selfishness. **The #1 killer of every relationship is selfishness.** Remember: it is a listening, and learning experiences that we can appeal, appreciate, and apply. If we become solely dependent upon our personal intellect, we can disrespect each other's significance. The most powerful weapon used to combat these types of issues, and the relationship demise is the **art of selflessness.** However, the weapon often used to encourage this confusion, separation, and in some cases yes divorce is the **act of "selfishness."** **There is a difference.**

If you individually, and collectively are not willing to **educate each other-examine your environment-empty some emotions- and evolve while doing it**. Then the quintessential value possibly will lose its strength. If you reject your partner's effort and refuse, to activate yours, there is a chance of producing and promoting the same results, because of the same approach. So many times we reap the same results, due to our laziness to recognize. This will only increase your repeated failed experiences. **Remember: repeated failed experiences only signifies lack of recognition. It didn't just start happening…you just never stopped it from happening.**

In this maturation stage the expectation must be higher, and the experience greater. **There can be no denial of warning signs. Remember there is always warning signs before failure.** If you get to this stage with the same old expectations, you ultimately limit your partner, yourself, and the depth of the relationship. **Remember: prior don't mean present, and present don't mean future.**

This does not rule out flaws, problems, and issues. However, is it strong enough to ruin your future? When there is the entry of selfishness, the motive never supports the unification. Do not get discouraged. **Every relationship at some point will struggle with the temptation of selfishness. It will either succumb to the onslaught, or survive it through timely recognition.**

Remember: **if there be no recognition of it...there may be no relationship because of it. If the relationship does not change this...the duration of the relationship will be challenge by this.**

My friend, selfishness often manifests itself, and gets its origin from a hurt history. Too many times selfishness discourages unity, while promoting disharmony. If the couple is failing to mature, and if no one is being, or willing to nurture; you can/ will possibly hurt the relationship from your past. I've notice in cases where one or the other felt the right, to maintain their rights without considering the rights of the other. Thereby, slacking on the preservation of the relationship. Couples have to be aware of this demon called "selfishness." It is: careless with feelings, it is emotionless, directly stubborn, and has a total disdain for agreement. **If you don't prepare for it...you will constantly be perplexed by it.**
One of the dangers that couples face going in, staying in, or leaving out: they expect their partner to tolerate a dysfunction, that they are not committed to changing. That is selfish. Remember: hurt people; hurt people with what they were hurt by. The hardest part of many relationships is trusting someone that you can feel comfortable enough to surrender your pain, weakness, and flaws. If you reject their support, you will inevitably suppress your pain, and expose someone to a bitter you,

rather than the better you. This is not just problematic… it is selfish. This is often used as arsenal, and a defense mode to suppress truth. **Are you ready for this**? **Sometimes you cannot erase the data, but you can begin to change the damage.**

This can only happen in a maturation stage. It is more than often the stigma of the last that hinders your success in a current one. If you are starting one, re-entering one; you must be strong enough, to be able to navigate through roadblocks that is experienced in every relationship. Ignorance to this: blocks future and adds stress to any resolve. One writer said: (unknown) "it is impossible to truly love without giving something away."

This stage is not all keeps. However, it is called sharing. **It is when couples commence to share that they release permission for each other to contribute in the experience.** If yesterday lingers you can prohibit access to the true essence of the relationship. This is why you have to know that you are ready. If not, your skepticism will subject you to constant frustration and limit your liberality. As we enter deeper into this chapter allow me to reveal some true essentials to building lasting and productive relations. **Are you ready?**

I have discovered in these 20 years with the same woman… **it takes work, to get the worth.** Through the bliss and the bleeding, and seeking the blessing, **it took us individually to decide a collective plan.** If we were going to be healthy, unselfish, productive **we** (repeat we) had to submit and surrender a sacrificial endeavor that chased, challenge and yet changed anything that would alter our plan. There must be a protection, and prevention plans, if you are to remain productive with each other and for each other. **Practice**

may not always make perfect. However it helps with prevention.

Please understand these essentials:
1. **The power of connection**
2. **The practice of agreement**
3. **The privilege of recovery**
4. **The procedure of forgiveness**
5. **The presence of unconditional love**

Are you ready?
These will provide a mutual edification and become beneficial as the relationship gains strength and momentum. They will also aid in the survival of your relations, and the revival of some emotions. If you are not, and have already rejected these principles, your relationship may not be ready for this stage. These are not immature, nor are they premature, that only depend on conditions, and reasons for belonging. This is for persons who understand, and are prepared to unconditionally apply, appeal, and appreciate the art of coming together and sharing something called a **"relationship."** Think about it... two individuals different, making up a connected strength. Wow! **Remember: you cannot stabilize as a couple, without effortlessly understanding and providing individual significance. The balance of the relationship hangs on the hinges of individual understanding, which gives value to who you are collectively. If you manipulate this...you will miss this.**

#1-Power of connection- let me ask you a question: if you are connected to them, then who are they connected to, or have been connected to? This is important. If you are not quite sure, you might need to consider going back to the first part of the book. The question may not to be who...but what spirit (attitude) ARE YOU CONNECTED TO? This is a mature stage. If you are panic picking, feeling impatient, haven't reflected, or have not made some modifications, then this is not your chapter. I will spend this chapter challenging you to take some knowledge test, of yourself and your significant or potential mate. Yes, for commonality, and compatibility purposes, but also how to promote harmony; that indicate your readiness. **Warning! Do not enter this lightly...**

This is not just about the sacred ceremony, but also the initial entry of any relationship. It is too often the issues we take for granted, that ends up grieving us the most. **The real power of connection is shown through the unselfish understanding of the individual you desire to be involved with. How separate you are without the violation and manipulation of your identity just proves how connected you can and will be.**

This has to be authentically unrestrained, unselfish, and unscripted. It should never be dominated driven by dictatorship. Nevertheless, it must be destiny driven to secure friendship, companionship, as well as partnership. One of the signs that the relationship is not connected or disconnecting is when someone tries intimidation by means to control it.

Let's look: sex – money- power- and yes religion, along with others are used to dominate intelligence over ignorance. **Until you remove the urge to promote the me, myself, and I in the relationship, you cannot, will not merge into a collaborate relationship.**

This cannot be the reclaiming of a separate identity…it must be the proclamation of your unity.

Warning!!! Do not allow these things to become problematic, or used as a means to manipulate choices. The reason for the disconnection is: we fail to prepare or practice against those things that continue to be our problems. The beauty of this connection is involved through developing knowledge, and an appreciation for interdependence. See: **independence only fosters a potential in the relationship. Interdependence focuses on the unified production of the relationship.**

Interdependence is:

- **Involving two or more**
- **Between among each other**
- **It is reciprocal**
- **Carried on between**
- **Shared by**
- **Existing among**

I think you get it… not selfish.

It independently, co-depends on each other's involvement. Your connection must guard what is close and that which is separate.

It is in this understanding that your connection: builds-encourages and shares the value of input.

To any young couples or those who have been hurt by or even in a current situations; interdependence must become a practice if the relationship will endure.

- Talk to each other- do not take for granted they know
- Share power equally- no dominance
- Be emotionally available
- Experience and expect good times

- **Invest in each other's vision**
- **Respect each other's difference**
- **Keep healthy boundaries**
- **Be realistic about resources**
- **Negotiate compromises**
- **Don't avoid arguments- they are healthy for the revelation as well as the growth for the relationship.**

If you battle with this your ability to connect, you will possibly create a disability. There are at least five strongholds that will combat your interdependence

1. The past
2. Your Money
3. Sex life- past/ present
4. Religion- preferences- convictions- dogmas
5. The tongue- MOUTH biggest one- not the least one

Your mouth carries with it compliments, and condemnation. It has the power of life and death concerning your relationship. It often disconnects, without guard or reservation of the damage it may cause. Once released intentionally or unintentionally, the severity of what has been said, can be an everlasting imprint, and intensify the disconnection. These things can cause such division in the relationship the connection suffers from the lack of understanding in who we are connecting to, and have been connected to. **Remember: it begins with the denial of self, and not the absence of self.** It is nothing wrong with having a strong mind in the relationship. This becomes challenging when disharmony becomes habitual, deliberately offensive, intimidating and demeaning. If not careful; your intellectual abilities, sexual expertise, your financial empowerment, your theological astuteness will

become offensive, and overbearing. **A selfish stimulation will always overrule an interdependent motivation.**
This will always encourage the relation trap. This is why interdependence needs to be magnified. If not, you will connect to autonomous attitude, while disconnecting from reliance on each other. My friend, survival comes with accountability. If you fail to hold each other accountable, you will be responsible for condoning confusion, and promoting disharmony. Your relationships grows healthier, and connects stronger by: emotionally, economically, ecologically, and moral reliance.
<u>Don't miss this!</u>
How can I accomplish this? It is through powerful connection. **Each couple must learn the art of being safe together. The very things that are hurtful to you individually...can become helpful to you collectively. Both persons must express the desire, and possess the ability to understand. Not feeling safe or, being safe within your connection, can increase the insufficient knowledge, and heighten the dissatisfaction in agreement. Pause...**

Q&A

- Do I understand edification/ and practice it?
- Do I listen for my partner's truth as well as acknowledge it?
- Am I empathetic?
- Are we prepared/ practicing self and mutual accountability?

Take time to answer these truthfully...
If any of these came back as a no, you must ask yourself the ultimate question.

162

Am I willing (self –accountability) to make any adjustments needed for the safety and the security of this relationship?

Now it is mutually important to hold your partner accountable.

Do not forget this as you are connecting.

Interdependence: is a relationship in which each member is mutually dependent on the other.

Don't miss this!

It is so important not to be intimidated or intimidating as you are connecting. You are forming a partnership that understands, and that is in touch with a spiritual connection, that leads to the ability to connect even in your differences. The more we make the effort to own our truth of who we are, and combine into a relationship with the significance of someone else; the greater the experience will be. If you are willing to trust your feelings with someone, or you are entrusting feelings currently, you are giving away something. **In every relationship: you must be prepared and positioned to give away some power over your feelings and well-being. This is why this stage is a maturation stage. You must still be aware of conscious choices, which make you solely responsible for the consequences. The healthiest connection is formed, when the opportunity is used not to harm the relationship with individual innuendos, which could cause a collective collapse. However, it's when you are able to distinguish interdependence over independence.**

This is why learning is essential, and readiness is not rushed. When there is the absence of learning each other, and forced inducement, the fortitude of your relationship could be in jeopardy. Are you willing to give/share some power over your well-being? Don't lose yourself in the process. However do not become lazy in finding the right connection. **It is essential to share the harmony, before becoming harmful to each other.** Remember independence only depends on self, and will not rely, or trust the availability of their partner. Can I help? **A personal condition does not always guarantee a powerful connection. This more than often determines the direction of the harmony or chaos of the relationship. The challenge comes when you are willing to surrender some individualism, for the shaping of what will be mutual beneficial. You do not lose identity...you gain the power of unity.**

One problem we have as couples in creating great connections, and great relationships; we try to go faster versus growing slower. Thereby, limiting our knowledge of each other. **Remember: part of growing... is you knowing. What is needed collectively?**

Ask the question/ wait for the answer.

1. Do I love / respect this person?
2. Do I trust this person?
3. Do I feel safe with this person?
4. Do I feel calm; Am I at peace with this person?

Now write your answers.

If you lack clarity… you may lack connection.
At this point: do not get offended by the answers you receive.
This is exposure to your partner's truth- you don't lose yours…you gain theirs. This is a progressive moment of truth. Do not be offended.
The pursuit for perfection is not as important as the prayer for progress.
Let's pray: Dear father, thank you for this place in the relationship where we can grow and be healthy for each other. Please give us the strength and the courage, not to operate selfishly in the confines of this relationship. Grant me the knowledge to know my partner, and connect without limitations to their significance. Thank you, for development, and growth that I desire. I ask for forward movement that is pleasing to you, for the advancement of our relationship. I
Refuse to retreat: emotionally, spiritually, financially, and physically. Thank you, for the success and the progress of this relationship. Amen.
Do not forget these as you connect:

- **Connect with yourself- your inner connection will affect an outer performance**
- **You must be a "can opener"- this means can you be available to hear and share in and with your mind and ears open attentively to your partner**
- **Learn a common love and trust- if not you will continue to fight with past pain, and control with selfish behavior**
- **Being here now- this can support proper placement. If you fail in being here, it could result in disconnecting from your partner, and never arriving to a common place. This could**

affect visibility issues with your partner (they can't see where they matter) being occupied with yourself, only confirms their belief of invisibility.

- Depict the core value in you and your partner- this is before you devalue who you pick as your partner. The more you mature in loving the things about your partner; the more you will become frustrated with the things that try to separate you from them. Sustain your partners ideas, that may not be favorable to you... but may builds a future together

- "Big one" value their vulnerability- these are mostly childhood triggers that trap the relationship. Sometimes your partner's withdrawals come from being withdrawn from. They only become habitual, when there is not an atmosphere conducive for change, trust and security. You must be aware. The environment that should have valued them...victimize them. You have the opportunity to make them feel valuable again. If you miss this; then the rebuttal to their withdrawal, will be one of your own.

- A house divided against itself will not stand (mark 3:25) it is your compassion that conquers in this connection.

- The preservation of any relationships is based upon the amount of respect that is mutually distributed.

- The way that you can tell that you are connecting is that there becomes a willingness to deny yourself, while seeking the better good of the one you are in relations with. The beauty of connecting to them and them to you; is that you become connectively inseparable. Real connection takes the practice of agreement.

- **There is no connection without agreement...**

#2-THE PRACTICE OF AGREEMENT

1. Agreement – Harmony or accordance in opinion
2. Mutual understanding

One of the greatest gifts to any relationship, marriage is the gift of agreement. Failing to come to agreement intensifies the conflict in any and all issues. This will always leave resolution at best stagnant, and worst the relationship dead. To my, new couples as well as old...disagreement is normal. It is when you allow your disagreement to rule over your chances of ever agreeing, that you give birth to your relationship struggles.

True agreement comes with a price. It is the price that calls for those in the relationship to surrender personal suggestions, for a connected truth. The consideration agreement brings you together. However, it is the committed agreement that keeps you inseparable. The relationship doesn't last if there is no committed agreement. This relationship that is committed to truth, survives any storm. *Luke 6:48 They are like a man building a house, who dug deep and laid the foundation on rock. When a flood came the torrent struck that house but could not shake it, because it was well built.* Say it! ANY STORM

Where there is agreement... there is power.

Mark 18:19- *that if two of you on earth agree about anything. You ask for it, it will be done.*

Agreement is your weapon for longevity.

- Provides unification
- Dispel and expel personal agendas, and motives
- Supports clarity

167

- Conforms to one truth
- Salutes mutual understanding, and celebrates mutual benefits

It is the practice and the presence of agreement that will eliminate confusion and contention. The reason why relationships are penalize is because the lack of practice. **The lack of practice, will forego the power of agreement, and its presence.**

The understanding of agreement says:

1. We will not be able to do this by ourselves or survive
2. We are different, creating a commonality
3. That Satan will always be in disagreement with our agreement
4. That God moves in the middle of agreement
5. That our agreement signifies order over chaos

To those considering marriage, recommitting to a relationship or have been damage by divorce. The enemy will always attack your agreement, and he will always praise your disagreement. He knows the first place to hurt any relationship is in the area called "agreement."

For so long we have been taught to concentrate on the similarities and not the differences. It is the very thing that makes us different, that enemy tries to use to prove our insignificance in the relationship. If **couples could ever reverse the psychology of this, they would be inseparable. It is knowing the differences, agreeing that you have them, not being intimidated by the challenges that come with those differences, that you are able to agree and present new similarities**. If not careful, the enemy of your mind will distinctively prove your idiosyncrasy and give birth to disagreement. **The deterioration starts when the disagreement never stops.** It's when either person is offended that the exposure creates a posture of negativity in the relationship. These offenses will be manifested in behavior that will not present or condone agreement. Once the offense comes, disagreement lingers. If the differences never recognize differences, then disagreement will keep doing what it started…division in the relationship. Exposing truth doesn't mean you are offending the relationship (it's received like this) it means there needs to be, and will be recovery through the practice of agreement.

Let me ask: what has been a common disagreement?

The only way to move from here is to agree that you have had, and are having disagreements, that you can't agree on. Make a list:

- Religion
- Money
- Children
- Friends
- Marriage
- Job
- Location

This list could go forever. The Talmud says: We do not see things as they are… We see things as we are.

Sometimes our common flaw is to trust that your partner is ok, without sufficient truth or agreement that would substantiate your opinion. **Assumption does not confirm agreement.**

If we just see things to our liking, they could cause the relationship exhaustion and not exhilaration. Do not forget this! Your agreement will jump-start: a new perspective is born, new possibilities are realized, re-discovery of attentiveness increases.

Do not become so caught up in your personal opinion, that you become incapable of liberating the relationship to its maximum potential.

How often do we as individuals in relationships, believe that our reality is the only reality?

This within itself limits learning, and teaches limits. Thereby, frustrating causing feebleness in the relationship.

If we begin to incarcerate our partner's perspective...we paralyze the progression of our relationship. It is when we attempt to manipulate each other choices; we ruin the chances, and forfeit the power of agreement. If not careful, you will fail in recognizing viewpoints; and become difficult and indifferent. Thereby, expecting your partner to surrender to your dominance. You cannot rely on your assumptions to control the individual views of your partner. News flash!!!! YOU ARE DIFFERENT...and that is ok. Yes, know the difference find the similarities.

This means:

- Genetically
- Socially
- Physiologically- psychologically-
- Historically

In saying this: you individually propose a plan, in which the relationship can collectively benefit from. Manipulation in most case: will only introduce intimidation, and induce an early termination to any relationship. **Sometimes the approach can, and will alter the agreement due to the**

anxiety, attitude, and aggressiveness for your partner to adjust to your truth.

When was the last time you agreed that your disagreements and were honest and true? This was without the control freak factoring in. CURVE BALL!!! Some problems may not be solved. Why? By the mere fact: of personal beliefs, perspectives and each other's convictions. This doesn't mean the relationship is over... is an opportunity for openness. This is why it's important to discuss and get clarity of perspectives before you become entrenched. **If there is a lack of openness, it possibly can discourage opportunity. Thereby, failing to unshackle the relationship.** Most people love their viewpoint, and will slightly consider others, if it offends their truth. My friend, offended truth creates a defensive person...even in the best relationships. People are not willing to surrender the truth, even if it means minimize your perspective. **Remember: assumption doesn't mean agreement.**

Answer this: how can two walk together unless they are in agreement?

It is imperative that you stay aware and alert to the areas that cause the most disagreements, and become responsive to possible solutions. If disagreements are causing dissension, then there are some questions I would like to ask you. Then ask yourself.

1. Why am I here?
2. How did I get here?
3. Why are we here
4. How did we get here?

Take time to answer these questions- what is the impact of your disagreement to the relationship? Discuss.

If you are married, thinking about it, been divorce, and reconsidering
Think about this:

- Is it a selfless relationship?
- Is it sacrificial?
- Is it sacred?

Clarity can be a tool used to stabilize what is apparently divided. So many times in our relationships; we either doubt our partner's knowledge or try to dictate their beliefs. This often will battle understanding, and extend the life of confusion to any relationship. I found out; **people who only live by their own conclusion, often times are insulted by what appears to be some else's view.** The offense will cause them to maximize their perceived strength, and attempt to immobilize your intellectual capacity. I also found out too many times people do not like to be wrong.

There are too many instances where agreement was available, but due to the ignorance of the partner to know the strength and intelligence of their mate, disagreement ruled. It ok if you don't know everything…that's the purpose of your partner. This is the beauty of agreement that you can harmonize as one, even when things are out of sync, someone can pick up the slack. This is what agreement does. You are coming together and harmonizing, to make one sound. This denotes oneness in the relationship, not found in a relation traps. There must always be awareness of where you stand, and your partner stand on issues that are pertinent to the relationship durability. What can you do if there is no resolve? It doesn't mean the end of the world, or the relationship. It may mean it's time for re-grouping, and re-focusing. Disagreement is not the opportunity to prove your personal

<u>point, by disqualifying theirs</u>. However, it sets the relationship up for introspection, and enlarging each other's perspective.

Let me ask:

- What does your relationship look like after disagreements?
- What are your normal disagreements/why?
- Have you considered your error?
- Does their truth matter? Have you clarified what they meant versus what you perceived?
- Do you speak truth/listen to truth? Accept their response.
- Have you both identified the problem and agreed that it is?
- Do you take ownership in the frustration cause in the relationship?
- Do you constantly sweat the small stuff?
- Have you tried practicing acceptance? Remember: you are not always right.
- Do you exercise patience?
- Have you considered that your expectations may be too high?
- Do you both desire harmony? Are you capable to leaving it in the past?

Your Answer

1.

2.

3.

4.

5.

6.

7.

8.

9.

10.

11.

12.

The importance in answering these questions; it will open you up with the things you have failed to know, and the things you need to know. We perish for the lack of knowledge. It is not because it is not available...we reject it when it is available. Your partner's truth is available, but often met with your resistance. Your resistance will never lead to the relationships revival.

PRACTICE AGREEMENT!!!!
Matthew 18:19- *if any two of you agree on earth concerning anything that they ask, it will be done*
If you are controlled by the disagreement, the disagreement will at some point prolong the conflict. Thereby, the conflict can and will make you desensitize to the solution.
If your relationships have been taunted by multiple disagreements, don't let the seemly insults isolate you from

each other. **Forcing yourself not to face facts can cause you to forego your future, and deprive you of a planned peace within your relationship.**

Please remember:

- Your assumption may not be their agreement
- Attempting to prove your personal points, can penalize the presence of agreement
- Be available to discuss, but also listen
- Do not rush the solution
- Listening is learning- not listening is laziness
- Do not make it about who wins the argument- rather how can we work to agree
- You must know your minimal effective response
- Have emotional closure
- Agreeing don't make them right, and disagreeing doesn't make you wrong- it opens the door for discussion

Always know the enemy #1 assignment against couples is to keep you from agreement...

Disagreement can cause a definite disconnect. Part of the maturation stage: is the ability to understand fallout, and having the capacity that causes renewal, that leads to recovery.

#3 The Privilege of recovery-

Part of recovery in relationships is link to how you can re-connect after fallout or fall away. **The privilege is afforded through re-evaluating what you once refuse to acknowledge.**

Can you bounce back from bleeding in the relationship? Facts:

- Recovery comes with the recognition of mutual deficiency – we both have issues within in the issue.
- Sensual activity does not always denote recovery…just maybe a temporary rectification that only satisfies a moment, does not signify a reconnected relationship.
- You cannot rush recovery.
- Recovery comes with blessings, also followed with boundaries
- Recovery is individual effort before it is collective practice
- Recovery is a remedy to demonic attacks
- Recovery is a part of healing, after hurting
- Recovery is a process, before a privilege- don't die in the process of recovery

One of the biggest issues that hinder relationships from bouncing back after a hit (every relationship has them) is the inability for one or both partner's to rescue the relationship after disconnecting. We fail in doing so, through closed dialogue. **So many times a closed mouth will also create a closed mind. If I fear the direction, we will fail in our reconnection.**

If fear and failure resides in our minds, the resistance will grow memories that will only concentrate on history. It is the resistance that remains, when we fail to recognize our personal responsibilities in rescuing the relationship, through reconnection and recovery.

Part of your revival, and you partners return is the power to assume that it is worth reconnecting and share in that like thinking. **Are you willing to improve on what you have been disapproving of, to stabilize what is needed for the reuniting of the relationship?** Another part of reconnecting is the revelation of your ignorance towards what is needed. Sometimes the admittance that you are not an expert will begin to start the reconnection experience. At this point: you cannot be condescending, arrogant that offends reuniting. Knowledge of your partner's readiness should create sensitivity to movement...that is a part of maturation.

Now you have to get to the core consciousness (sense of self). What's going on with me will begin to extract some of the pressure, of what going on with us (equally important). Relationships take a hit due to each individual not spending adequate time on understanding their self-worth. **How you relate to yourself is an important component of how not to keep enduring by yourself. The right questions to yourself; can start the right discussions with your mate. Your recovery begins in your ability to not only see, but to comprehend the worth of who you are to the relationship.**

Do you know who you are to the relationship?

Do you have an idea of what you possess?

Are you link to someone who adds value to what you already have?

Proper reconnection will take place as both parties take a critical look at the spirit in which you approach and function within the parameters of the relationship.

Be careful of extended disconnection that will never let you consider recovering. Extended disconnecting comes from events causing prolong periods of misery, shame, and even guilt from life issues. Thereby, giving in to a defense mechanism that resides internally. You will connect to people physically, without returning to yourself fully. You pre-judge situations, that you make any relationship partial, and withdrawn. Be careful right here. **You can become so disconnected after an offense, that you will become preoccupied with your hurt, and you will prioritize hurt over healing. Can you recover after you have discovered, that very thing that was uncovered, and manifested the exposure to your hurt?**

In most cases the severity of the situations become abrasive and abusive to both parties. At this point: we will fail in approach and function of our relationship. The question is on the table…Can you recover, from what you have discovered?

Signs you may not want recovery:

- Fail to seek time to recover
- Other things, or people have your attention- easily distracted by
- Making your partner a lower priority
- Poor listener- looking for reasons to disagree
- Having a defensive wall up to combat truth
- Not responding to matters/ issues concerning your mate
- Big one- infidelity
- Judging, criticizing, or shaming
- Expect sensitivity to your feelings- reject your partner's
- Selfish – everything about you
- Addictions
- Incessant complaining (never ceasing
- Demeaning or belittling your partner
- A taker of time not a giver

Question: can you recover from what you have discovered?

If there is going to be privilege...there must be practice.
Part of many couples frustration in attempting to recover is there's no validation from each other. You must include them in the process, and they must include you. If relationships are going to exemplify the example, they must intensify the execution.

Be patient- don't push
Be meek- not arrogant
Be accountable- not judging everything
Be confident- not provoking
Be open- not secluded
Be direct- but not offensive

To recover you must be willing to become recommitted, to recreating what was united you in the first place. After you recreate the unity, then reclaim each other's trust and faith in the relationship. This process will help you with the reconciliation to take place. The reconciliation, and the reconsideration
will help expedite the recuperation. The recuperation helps seal the reconnection. If you don't recover with this person, (try hard) do not abandon the right and the privilege to reconcile with yourself?

CAN YOU RECOVER FROM WHAT YOU HAVE DISCOVERED? ANS. NO YOU CANNOT IF YOU ARE NOT WILLING TO FORGIVE...

#4THE PROCEDURE OF FORGIVENESS-
The procedure- synonymous with:

- Practice
- Process

- Method
- Course of action
- System
- Formula
- Route

Let's see:

1. How will you practice through a pain that you seemly can't process?
2. How long will this process (development) be?
3. What method or course of action should be taken against this offense?
4. Have you manufactured a mental precautionary system/ formula to combat the pain?
5. What route will you take after the offense?

Of forgiveness:

Wikipedia dictionary- The intentional and voluntary process, by which a victim undergoes a change of feelings and attitude regarding an offense, let's go of negative emotions such as vengefulness, with an increased ability to wish the offenders well.

Griertionary- The act or process, where you no longer hold one hostage or guilty/ responsible, that caused the hurt, pain, grief, or shame. You remove/ release the burden from the offender.

ARE YOU READY?

ONE OF YOUR BIGGEST BATTLES IN ANY RELATIONSHIP IS THE EMOTIONAL AND PYSCHOLOGICAL REMOVAL OF THING THAT RENDERS THE MOST PAIN, AND PARDON THE OFFENSE IN ORDER FOR THE RELATIONSHIP TO MOVE FORWARD, MATURE, AND REGAIN MOMENTUM. PART OF THE PROCESS IS BEING

ABLE TO GO THROUGH THE PROCEDURE THAT IS NECESSARY FOR THE HEALING.

In a conversation with my wife we begin a subject matter on forgiveness. It was a general conversation, which became very profound in its nature. It's in our transparency to each other, that we attempt to keep it real with people. The only way we have been able to survive some of our greatest test is through the procedure of forgiveness. **Where we made up in our minds individually, to survive collectively.** If we were to move past the place of our hurt, pain, disappointments, we could not hold each other hostage, by way of reminder to the offense. As we discuss the matter, she stated by way of observation; **that real forgiveness moves past verbalization, and becomes obvious through action.** If it is not depicted in character, then the lack of authenticity diminishes the growth of the relationship.

Q&A

Do you constantly remind them of the offense towards you?

How many times should you forgive them?

How many times have you forgiven?

Why do keep forgiving the same thing?

Take time to answer these.

I also asked my wife; why is it that people fail to forgive in their relationship? She stated: so many times people have a plan, but do not practice it. They know what to do; but to perform and process it in their stage of hurt doesn't seem practical. They will expect it from you, but are not willing to surrender it. Thereby, causing stunted growth, a divided relationship, it also allows the enemy to present adversarial entries to and through your mind. This diverts the relationship from strength to struggle.

Have you considered a lot of our ailments, especially in our relationships; are due to the things that we fail to release. The question has to be: why we want forgive?

Reasons:

1. We don't value the relationship
2. We become afraid of perception (signs of weakness, and vulnerability)
3. Pride- (it always come before the fall)
4. We don't like the process
5. We have trained ourselves to hold on, and not release
6. My revenge takes precedence over my forgiveness

My friend, there is no true freedom without the power, the practice, and the presence of forgiveness. It can begin to affect health, management of conflict resolution, and even your spirituality. Your thought process begins a negative decline, and rebels against any type of restoration. Be careful right here. If you fail to seek forgiveness, you possibly can sacrifice the relationship essentials. This is due to selfish –interpretations. You may unintentionally reach out to an outside source, which may cause you to betray your relationship, and fall for a relation trap.

It always appears, as a remedy never anticipate that it would be reckless. That which you don't fix... you often fight. That, which you constantly fight... you will scarcely forgive. That, which you seek not to forgive, you will possibly forfeit the relationship

Thereby, be subjected to the scrutiny of self- abuse and pressure that comes with your deliberation.

Ask yourself:

- Can I let go the desire to hold on to it?
- Am I holding to a previous resentment?
- Has the pain or the pressure shown up in my present relationship?
- Have I built a wall that houses my anger, and bitterness?

Facts:

- Forgiveness is about you
- Forgiveness is not about another person perception
- Forgiveness offers and free expectation
- Forgiveness provides a way to deepen your relationship with yourself and with others
- Forgiveness allows restoration to begin

Do not become so stubborn that you refuse to express your thoughts, or you refuse to forgive the one that help initiate the expression. The silence can and will denote unforgiveness.

Every relationship will at some point have to battle with forgiveness. The thought of dealing with certain offenses is heart- wrenching, but necessary. **Forgiveness doesn't mean toleration. However, it sets up the opportunity for restoration, and recovery.** This is a chance to move forward from events that will otherwise keep you bound…if you allow it. **STOP RIGHT HERE!!!! SAY IT. I NEED TO FORGIVE.**

WHAT HOLDS YOU UP, AND THE RELATIONSHIP IS THE FORCE OF UNFORGIVENESS...

My friend, if the relationship or your individual life is going to proceed, you cannot harbor (give strength) to **that** anymore. Pause. (This may be the hard part. It was for me.)

LET'S PRAY...

Dear father help me with the things that I can't let go. I want to move on, I want to forgive. I admit I am struggling with these issues. I admit the pain and the pressure is hard to bear. I need your strength, and your guidance. AMEN

I remember praying this. I DID NOT WANT TO FORGIVE...BUT HAD TO.

I realized that my pain was real. However, **my revenge couldn't be my restoration**. Just as what was done to me was (to me) unforgivable; my unforgiveness (to God) was unforgivable. Remember: in the Lord's Prayer (Matthew 5)- forgive us of our trespasses as we forgive those who trespass against us. It is contingent. Matthew 18:35- how can I forgive you, if you will not (paraphrase). The strength of forgiveness in our relationships overrides the struggle. **This doesn't mean condoning on your part...it means conditioning. Remember: forgiveness is about you.**

If you can cover over an offense, you will promote love. If you choose to continue in your unforgiveness, then you separate the repair. Proverbs 17:9

One of the biggest entanglements of couples; is not being able to get pass resentments. Not getting pass...keeps you lock in the past. This is in return causes your present to become just as your past.

You must choose whether to forgive or not. **If you are going to forgive, you cannot determine if they deserve it** or not. To fluctuate in choice is to frustrate the future of the relationship. It is not a feeling, but a decision. If you hold on to a feeling...you may never feel. Be careful!!! Change is not always the outcome...but a change will come over you.

Say it with me. I must choose to forgive...

Q&A

1. Do you allow your partner the opportunity to express themselves, or have your perception overtaken every matter? Thereby causing unforgiveness?

Unforgiveness often rules and ruins because of the resentment in relational communication. When communication becomes complicated, then forgiveness is frustrated by perception. Too often the intentions are misinterpreted, and create feelings of resentments that are not easily forgotten, or easily healed. **If each party fails in their responsibility in mutual understanding, and mutual edification, the relationship becomes conducive for misunderstanding, and unforgiveness.**

Remember: either it's a selfish act or a selfless act.

Take a min:

What are the positives of your partner? Have you told them vs. finding fault?

What are the negatives of you? Have you come to grip with them?

What are the potentials of the relationship? Have you pursued them?

Answer

1.

2.

3.

What did you discover? Discuss

If you stay stuck in the fact that you can't let go...you want let go.

So many times we feel we have the right to feel the way we do. In return we: disregard any other feelings, and require punishment as a means to of restitution for our pain. To most couples this is an awkward place. This awkward place becomes a disassociated place, and a divided place. The relationship that now needs healing; the unforgiveness disallows the momentum. If your mind, which controls the attitude, feels confined by circumstances, it will not release a pardon. Some relationships are dominated by the things are considered unforgivable; and often used as an arsenal, to manipulate agendas. Be careful!!!

As much as we pretend that they don't bother us, and we are over it; our behavior often contradicts that fact. I have seen in too many cases, where the suppression of feelings, along with the camouflage of emotions were hidden, until someone felt their perceived rights were violated, and exposed their inner convictions. So many times this is the danger of starting new relationships or revenge relationships. There is no real confession, to your suppressions. The saddest part: someone has to be the recipient of what you didn't fix, but want him or her to face. Or they become a convenience in the midst of consequences, and circumstances. GET FREE... FORGIVE!

Q&A

What is holding you back?

Don't become so isolated and separated, that you become withdrawn emotionally. When relationship arrives here the selective amnesia plagues the definition of who you are, and what the relationship could, and should be.

- You will reduce expressions of love
- The relationship will become, and remain rigid
- Having a readiness of criticism, and anticipated contention
- You will become suspect of everything about your relations

Nelson Mandela says: *"resentment is like drinking poison and then hoping it will kill your enemies."*

My friend, don't allow your unforgiveness to become your safety net. **The procedure of forgiveness is giving power back to a relationship that faced possible termination.** It simply gives it momentum.

Pain will always shows up to prove to you, or remind you of a slight chance of healing. The practice and procedure reminds you how the healing has started. Even though incremental, it is further than where you were.

Say it, God heal me beyond where I am currently...

The strength of the relationship is how you can get pass the struggle. This was my issue. I did not want to leave the place of anger, bitterness, resentment, or revenge.

187

I needed someone to feel like I felt. To me: that was the right way to feel. **Remember: resentment will make restoration rigid**. No one wins when pain is left unresolved. Pain has a way releasing insensitivity. When you or your mate becomes insensitive the turmoil-chaos-disorder-confusion-uproar-mayhem-commotion- the havoc increases. Thereby, causing a lack of support, constant misunderstandings, and unmet expectations. These all are signs of revenge and resentment. They will not pursue a remedy, and the relationship does not find restoration. **Say it...I must promote forgiveness in my relationship.**

Q &A

1. Can you move pass this point?

    1. Have you tried?

    2. If you can't why?

Remember: one of the biggest reasons we don't move is our pride. Your pride will hold on to what it feel is necessary to harbor, that gives strength to its reason. Do not allow the event of yesterday to become your weapon for tomorrow. If not careful...YOUR PAST WILL BECOME YOUR FUTURE.

This may not change everything. However, these will change something.

- Acknowledge that you hurt or are hurting
- Ask for forgiveness
- Apologize for your part
- Allow the necessary adjustments to take place as they take time
- If at all possible make amends
- When unforgiveness is present, the absence of forgiveness can extend your grief.

Remember: I told you I did not want to change how I felt. Because, I did not want to change my feelings…my feelings start changing me. It extended my grief, and prolonged my freedom. The forgiveness was a major part of my solution. I gave permission to unforgiveness to be my stumbling block. What I thought I had remedied; I found myself reviving. So instead of you finding value in the relationship, you will victimize it. **Be careful right here. You will have multiple relational stains, because of no memory stoppage. The reminders of the offense, will cause you to have intentions, but overwhelmed by the struggle of memory. History and memory are the most powerful nemesis to restoration. The lesson of the pain will not permit you to listen or embrace the practice and procedure of forgiveness.**

Tim, I want to. You have to. This is not demanding, it is a part of your deliverance. Remember: this is about you, and not their perception.

Forgiveness doesn't look to balance a situation to see if it is fair. It just doesn't allow the pain to take root.

Sometimes the deeper the love, and the deeper the hurt, the harder the forgiveness will be.

How hard has it been to feel the pain, and begin to refocus on the relationship?

Journal here:

A moment- how did you feel?

A memory- what experience did you gain?

True to yourself.

Let's be true:

- This requires a willing me- beyond my pain, beyond my injury
- (Big one)- I must recognize at some point they had some pain, that cause me some pain, right or wrong my forgiveness is my release and part of their healing
- If I don't release or forgive- I give permission to the re-enactment. It may not be the same person; it could be the same spirit (attitude).
- Forgiveness cost something…it is called denial.

My friend, forgiveness has no limits. Can anything be forgiven? Yes, just doesn't have to be tolerated. **Remember: this is not about condoning…it is about conditioning.**

Please, take time to recognize the real enemy in the relationship. You cannot, nor will be able to effectively fight the battle without identifying why the relationship has arrived here. True relationships, and marriages are targets for this enemy. He programs an event, he looks for participants, he deludes the participant, he attacks the partner using the participant as bait, he flees and leave you and the relationship damaged, he praises the fact of potential separation, and or divorce, now you have the ultimate choice to make forgiveness an option, or use unforgiveness as arsenal.

- Ridicules
- Taunts
- Utilizes pain as a resolve
- Victimizes

- Worries – never yields to what is right- creates a zeal for your hurt

Every relationship at some point will deal with some type issue that will require forgiveness Warning!!! Do not be ignorant to the devices of the devil that causes deception to be the foundation of your unforgiveness.

This is not that you have become oblivious to a reality and numb to your pain (it hurt) - you have just begun to check those things that would devour and divide you from God's forgiveness.

Pause... I know you hurt, but heal through your forgiveness.

- After the infidelity
- After the suicidal thoughts
- After the hospitalization
- After the murderous attitude

What was practiced with my mouth wasn't purposed in my heart. I had to start the procedure, and go through the process of forgiveness. I had to make up in my mind (you will to) that I would not stay a victim to my dis may. However, became vulnerable to anticipation for the revitalization of my belief in my relationship. I did not have to be vindictive. The road to not only my healing started, but the relationship would revolve.

Unforgiveness only sets you up for painful memories- torn relationships – broken hearts- and no reconciliation. **If you can't forgive for the reconciliation of the relationship...do it for the revitalization of your mind. Remember: this is about you. Think about it:**

- If you have been hurt make a list of wounded you. Whether living or dead, have you taken it to a relationship with you, does it reside there now? Has

191

it been a part of every relationship you have attempted to have, and every decision-making? Remember they don't have to be there to do the damage. The thought has to be available.

- Ask God to forgive you of holding grudges- ask how to remove the offense from your heart- ask him how to cleanse your thoughts- renounce the spirit of unforgiveness
- Begin the procedure of forgiving each offender- if you retain one you possibly detain all.
- Forgive them verbally- specifically-BIG ONE
- Ask yourself do I want to live in this and under this pressure for the rest of my life?
- What have I lost or losing because I refuse to release them and myself?
- Is this really worth me damaging my spirit?
- Has this become my stronghold?
- Will my relationship or relationships continued to be hindered by me?
- BIG ONE- try and command blessing, where you demanded demise.
- Unforgiveness:
- Attacks
- Baffles
- Confrontational
- Demonic
- Edgy
- Frustrates
- Hinders
- Irritates
- Justify anger
- Kills joy
- Lust for revenge

- Manipulate
- Never forgives
- Oppresses-
- Punishes people- paralyzes relationships
- Stays in a Quandary

The momentum comes from the maturation of the heart of the persons involved. This is not just a requirement; it has to be about a relinquishment.
Things to remember:

1. There is an individual and collective victory over bitterness, resentment, and anger
2. I realize I need forgiveness myself
3. The truth be told- there are some things I have not disclosed, whether, thought or deed- and I refuse to enter into a agreement with Satan by not forgiving
4. That God has tolerated and covered me in my secrets
5. There are no big and little ones…all are offenses
6. There has be a time to excuse the penalty for the offense- my responsibility
7. I must renounce the resentment if I am looking for restoration
8. I have a choice- but it is also my chance
9. I don't want to hinder God's movement in my life
10. It is part of my maturation and my momentum
11. It is the redeemer and the restorer of my relationship
12. You must love yourself more than your yesterday pain

No it doesn't mean toleration…it means maturation. When you learn it; you can live it. However, you can't live it… if you don't unconditionally love it.

#5. THE PRESENCE OF UNCONDITIONAL LOVE

I truly believe, as we come to a close of this journey, that there is no relationship safe and secure, neither is there endurance without the **presence of unconditional love. If you lack in this... chances of survival is very slim.** There is no real connection- practical agreement- chance of recovery- true forgiveness, without the presence and the prevailing gift of unconditional love.

Long lasting relationships require unconditional love. Do not get it confused with co- dependent love. **Co-dependent** says that you will attempt to meet all the needs, to accept and overlook all of the partner's behaviors and actions no matter how selfish or demanding. **Unconditional** is grounded in a healthy foundation of self-respect and respect for the individual sharing the relationship with you. However, it begins with you. You must have (repeat- I must have) a strong sense of self-esteem and self- confidence. This does not negate the fact of insufficiency, and difficulties or the need for attention. It denotes a feel good about yourself attitude, and the kind of qualities you bring to the relationship. **You cannot release to another person...what you have not first offered to yourself.**

If you are insecure in this area, you could have a great impact on the mutual happiness of the relationship. Say this...the best thing I could ever do for my relationship is love myself.

Pause.

Now say it again!!! The best thing I could do for my relationship is love myself.

Now the part of this relationship that you are responsible for is ready for you, and you are ready for it...unconditionally

Unconditional love has to be able to love the other person as they are in their essence, (core, heart, fundamental nature) and their uniqueness. The part that moves you is: seeing your value, your capacity, and standing with it in confidence. If you do the relationship survives. Nevertheless, if you don't the relationship suffers. Once again this is not about someone being an extension of you, this is about you being able accept and view his or her individual uniqueness. This comes: with accepting yours, and celebrating. **For both to experience it, both have to participate in it.**

Remember: lasting relationships require unconditional love.

When this kind of love can be shared with no restraints; the privilege to release it, and receive is a phenomenon. Dr. Jeremy Nicholson (personality psychiatrist and relationship consultant) *says "it is your job in the relationship to use your influence in a caring and disciplinary manner to create a balanced exchange with your partner."*

My friend, unconditional love should release a mutually beneficial and satisfactory partnership.

This is not the absence of issues... it is just the presence of unconditional love.

I have seen it in action. It can produce bountiful blessings in a relationship. It should nonetheless promote personal boundaries in and none threatening way. When couples determine to communicate- negotiate- and make the necessary adjustments; that couple begins to build a strong relationship. This is not manipulated love; it is mature unconditional love.

Let's talk:

What is the health of the relationship?

Do you have a working partner?

Are you guys communicating?

Are you committed? Or are you comfortable?

Are both parties cooperative?

Ans. Honestly-

Remember: if both going to experience it...both must participate in it.

If you don't blend together you will bleed individually. Think about it:

- **Is it possible to love without limits and still have contingencies placed on the relationship?**
- **Should you have to tolerate certain behaviors to prove you unconditional love?**

Yes, unconditionally we seek the better good, it doesn't indicate lowering standards. It is because you love that you motivate, and seek for the best for them, and for/ from you. This is the place: where the reciprocation, and identification of a conscious partner not only gravitates, but participates in the relationship.

Be careful right here... Too many times we fail in this vital and pre-cautious area. We try to make our partners earn it. We manipulate them earning on the basis of conscious or

196

unconscious conditioning being met. In other words...do it my way, and it will go or not go. Should there be contingencies?

The real power of love is catching the essence of the one who is extending it. If they are or you are made to prove it, then the authenticity stands to be questioned. Unconditional love must be primary not secondary.

Facts:

If it is conditional it is not love...

Conditional love will always demonstrate the need for personal gratification to be maintained.

It is only produced by what is presented to them and for them, not what is practiced by them.

Unconditional love is required for long lasting relationships.

C.G. Jung was a Swiss psychiatrist and psychotherapist who founded analytical psychology says *"Seldom or never does a marriage develop into an individual relationship smoothly without crisis. There is no birth of consciousness without pain."*

Remember: the beauty of enjoying your relationship collectively is how you educate, and experience each other individually. This does not make it an individual relationship. However, it opens each person up to a greater identity of each other.

My, friend we cannot become so rejected by our own identity in the relationship that we fail to be enlightened by that, which is willing and able to make us conscious. I know the truth hurts. It also sets you free.

In his book Getting the love you want- A Guide for Couples DR. Harville Hendrix says in one of the ten characteristics of a conscious marriage- *"you realize your love relationship has a hidden purpose. You learn to recognize the unresolved issues that underlie certain desires and needs. Daily interactions take on more meaning."*

My friends, don't miss this…

The power and the presence of this conscious love allow you to begin making sense, and start gaining control. Through positive recognition, and awareness ignorance diminishes.

If you are always clueless, and or dominated by what you see, it may interrupt the harmony, and the essence of what you cannot see. Remember: it must appeal, be appreciated and be applied for the endurance of the relationship.

Sometimes the overwhelming need to be loved will cause an exaggerated attitude to be shown, as if the love already exists. It is the unconscious fabrication that holds up the conscious truth. This kind of love is not reaction…it is a reality. It is not a means to accept everything as right. It is when you begin to discover the wrong; that you don't consider it to be an opportunity to withhold forgiveness, compassion, or a emotion that seek the better after you have been expose to the worst. Even in the times of much needed solitude, can you validate, and give priority to your detachment (sometimes you need breathing room)? This must be done without deliberately offending, due to an isolated emotion in the moment.

Don't fool yourself. There are times where your love will fail to meet the imperatives- certain conditions. It at this point their needs/ wants and preferences may be affected by unmet expectations. Does this qualify or disqualify them from your love?

Your capacity to love regardless, doesn't affect your consciousness of the relationship. It is just determined to not die, even if the relationship is down.

Unconditional love cannot be extended unless it is resonate in you. It is called Self-Acceptance. This comes without reservation or restrictions. I recognize my weakness and limitations. This does not interfere with my ability to accept myself. This is still a part of the maturation stage. **(Please do this)** I spend more time exploring the parts that I have not been able to accept about myself. As you begin this journey: you find out the more acceptance in the relationship.

When you are able to get a clear perspective on these matters, you will lessen the ambivalent attitudes, and errant behaviors that were once unrestrained. This becomes climatic in its nature. The fact: that someone could truly love you without restrictions is somewhat preposterous. Nevertheless to experience is profound and breathtaking. **Can you really accept this? Have you experience this? The problem may not be in them accepting you. Have you accepted you? The power of you accepting you is being able to release that love to someone else. The true art of self- acceptance is the action that comes with unconditionally loving another. As you and your mate come together, the love helps you to commune together. It's not an act...it's an action.**

Are you ready for this????

This kind of love is a mature love. This does not mean that the relationship is perfect, flawless, without frustration, never depressing, argument free of course not. It doesn't mean stupidity. It's just mean you have taken on a mature

identity. Let's not get it confused. This is not **unconditional dedication- this refers to an act irrespective (despite) your feelings. I.e. –you fill or consider that you have to stay because of, by some duty. Unconditional love- is act of feelings irrespective of will- it separates you from your behaviors. So I don't stop loving you, I take on an understanding of relationship modifications, necessary for the relationship's maturation.**
Let's see:

- What is your visualization of love?
- Do you/ have you taken time to visualize your partner?
- Do you/ can you refine the image to see them as whole and spiritual beings?
- How can help the wounds that you were unaware of, but now are privy?
- Do you expect relational healing in the weak areas?
- Do you imagine/ expect the same energy coming back, as being released?

Ans. Be true
The powerful of this true love is hidden, until it is exposed. Now both parties are responsible for maintaining their revelation. My friend, you cannot love like this, unless the love of God resides in you.
This love:

- Gives the best, even when experiencing wrong
- It doesn't demand that you earn it
- It does not give up
- You don't just do it…you become it.

There are circumstances where they may not receive your love, shown through their actions. That does not mean you refuse to show it through your reactions.

This kind of love is the glue to every potential, productive, and positive relationship. The only real requirement is that you deny yourself. It is the sticktoitness that is able to combat a lethargic attitude towards this essential ingredient for your relationship.

- It brings agreement
- It continuously connects
- Respects the privilege of recovery
- It supports the process of forgiveness
- It presents itself unconditionally

Talk to me.

1. What have been your struggles with love?
2. Do you present unconditional love?
3. Do you believe that you are lacking?

Part of the maturation of the relationship is to arrive to truths to these questions, for they are link to your relationship destiny.

Unconditional love challenge- Sometimes you will be ask to solve problems you didn't cause. Or challenge to stay when the conditions are certain that it is time to go. Remember: conditions often will not allow you to see the need to present unconditional love.

To my couples, potential couples, clueless people trying to make sense, the problem that has been hindering, or has hindered the development of your relationship and growth is summed up in the conditions that come with your love.

Conditions:

- Broken focus
- Bound and baffled by facts

- Will not bargain for the relationship's future

If your relationship is contingent upon conditions for the survival…it will not survive

Warning!!!

If you are made to qualify for it… it is not love. You are supporting someone else's lust.

- Love doesn't demand qualification, just dedication
- It is not in a certain category, it is absolute
- It is unreserved, no restrictions
- It is sacrificial
- It is selfless

Who we are to each other extends pass conditions on to our commonalties. So we appeal, appreciate and apply it to the destiny of our relationship.

Your destiny-

- This cannot be delusional it must be deliberate
- It is designed by God, but often diluted by man
- It understands in marriage, it is for better or for worst. Not, when it gets worst, I look for better
- You cannot enter into your relationship destiny lightly
- Destiny- is revelation, not conditional
- It is never insensitive, impulsive or impatient
- It is not assumed, it is accurate
- This has to prevalent (established) if the relationship is going to relevant.
- Igniting passion- how deep is your love?
- Impacting personally- do they really know the depth
- Implementing purposefully- why do you love so much- what is the intent behind it.

Remember: love is a choice and also a chance.

Unconditional love:

1. Chooses to forget
2. Chooses to reconcile before revenge
3. It doesn't wait to delete wrongful facts, it takes the power away to not forfeit the future
4. It does not rejoice in someone else's demise
5. It endures all things
6. It believes and hope all things
7. It keep moving even when life cause it to stand still
8. It sees vulnerability as an honorable strength, not dis-honorable weakness
9. If the relationship has an incomplete understanding, each individual can potentially misrepresent the true value, and the true love needed. It is the presence of unconditional love that proves the possibility and power of a long lasting relationship. This goes far pass humanistic ideology. It is not only an identity…in releases a liberality in the relationship.

Even if your relationship expires (we hope not) the beauty of exploring, and accepting parts about you, that were not at one time comprehensible, has made the experience more educating and preparatory for the next. Part of interpreting this love: sets precedence, and a positive reinforcement to the unrestricted love within your relationship.

Remember: how you meet and how you live together will constantly be tested. That is why we say, "Love endures all things.

Francois Duc de la Rochefoucauld a 17th century French author and moralist stated, *"True love is like ghosts which everybody talks about and few have seen."*

My friend if it is just about warm feelings, physical attractions, and sexual activity, we all may be in trouble. My Big Mama use to say, "You better know what you getting yourself into. **Anybody** can say a thing... everybody can't do it. Talk is cheap if you don't have no action."

Do me a favor ask yourself, and then asks your partner, is there something wrong with the way I/ we love? Please, remember: God is the key to this type of love, the main reason relationship fail in this area, because there is no God to guide. **Misunderstanding will rule where A GOD TO GUIDE doesn't reside.**

After I had tolerated and accepted misunderstanding so long (talk about it- didn't experience it) it became my desire to practice and produce a God kind of love in my relationship. Remember: trust in the lord with all your heart and lean not to your own understanding, but in all your ways acknowledges him, and he will direct your relationship's path. **When you position yourself to your thinking, make sure it doesn't plummet the relationship to start sinking. I will agree staying is not always the solution. Will running always be your remedy?**

This wasn't just about my emotion; this resided in my heart. The truth about emotions: is they more than often fluctuate, leaving you hopeless and empty. EMPTY EMOTIONS DO NOT CARRY UNCODITIONAL LOVE. **Conditional love mixed with empty emotions is a recipe for disaster and misdirected obligations**. Be careful!!! You will become more responsible to respond to an emotion, than reliable to the love in the relationship. This may render you rigid results.

This can and will in most cases cause major issues. Why? The requirement of the condition rendered by you or your mate, may render competition versus compatibility. RELATIONSHIP OR TRAP?

Repeat this- if we are going to complete this, we cannot compete for this.

Warning!!! As long as conditions exist, the relationship will possibly face an exodus.

This may start out unintentionally, if not fixed it will become customary.

- How many times have you stayed just because of the conditions?
- Are you still there?
- What were the conditions?
- Did you expect them or accept them?

Do not get the expression of how you feel confused with the essence of fulfilling the relationship. Thing and expressions cease, it is the true love that will endure.

The Emotional love you trusted might not be the enduring love you can trace.

Most times even in marriages we only have lust, and not true love. Be careful, not to build your relationships around emotions, and not endurance. The desire may disappear, and so will the relationship. If it is godless it will hasten to become emotionless. If it is Godly, it will find a way to endure all things. The late Dr. Myles Munroe declares in his book: The power of Love and Marriage. That function determines design, and design determines need. Each individual has a different need in the relationship. This is because they are designed differently. (Paraphrase)

Tim Grier says, because the design is different...the diagnosis and the degree of love must be.

This is how you true love warrants the unconditional action reserved for each other. That you are capable of distinguish the need, and supplying without restraints, or restrictions for the relationship.

Remember: needs vary and the love aids in sustaining them.
Let's see:

MAN NEEDS	WOMAN NEEDS
SEX	AFFECTION
COMPANIONSHIP	COMMUNICATION
ATTRACTION	HONESTY AND OPENNESS
PEACE IN THE HOME	FINANCIAL STABILITY
RESPECT/ADMIRATION	COMMITMENT

BOTH NEED
UNDERSTANDING AND UNCONDITIONAL LOVE TO SUSTAIN THE RELATIONSHIP

Finding a true love is not a notion it becomes your nature. You don't need a reason...when they are
Remember: notions create conditions – conditions create expectations- expectations create routines- routines create too often disappointments – disappointments lead to failed relationships- and divorced marriages.

Challenge: DAILY REFRESH YOUR LOVE
This type of love is not all personal it is all-present.
If you reject it- refuse to relinquish it you run the risk of a relation trap. Is it a relationship or another relation trap?

You will become:

- Uncertain

- Uncured
- Uncomfortable
- Uncommitted
- Unconcerned
- Unfaithful
- And ultimately Unfit
- This leaves the possibility of a prosperous relationship Unfortunate
- Just try unconditional…

Your Conditions are not comfortable neither will the relationship.
Remember:
Love is patient
Love is kind
It does not envy
It does not boast
It is not proud
It does not dishonor
It is not self –seeking
It is not easily angered
It keeps no record of wrong doings
It does delight in evil but rejoices in truth
It always protects – it always trust- always hopes- always preserves- it never fails
Because it never fails… your relationship do not have to fall.

ARE YOU READY?

THINGS TO REMEMBER:

- The location of your mind determines the liberation of your heart
- That stupidity is not a requirement. However its always optional
- The worse kind of abuse is self-abuse
- Do allow impatience to pressure your pick, for it will pick your pressure.
- Do not rush readiness
- It takes work to get worth
- Being safe together is being secure in your individuality. Each couple must learn to be safe together
- Your relationship must be able to provide and accept individual significance
- The preservation of any relationship is based upon the amount of respect that is mutually distributed
- The biggest agreement in any relationship, is the agreement that you are different creating similarities
- Do not allow your personal views to be aggressively insensitive to your partners perspective
- Insensitivity to your partner could ruin the maximum potential of the relationship
- Don't allow rejection to become a way of expectancy
- Let rejection become a hurdle not a hindrance
- If you don't trust what is inside of you, you will forever live in indeciveness
- It not what people put you through, it is what you permit.
- Convenient doesn't always secure connection
- Either running is a reality or staying is a solution
- Modify changes, do not multiply dysfunctions

- If you can't forgive for the reconciliation of your relationship, do it for the revitalization of your mind
- How you meet and how you live together will always be tested
- Misunderstanding will rule where there is no God to guide to reside
- If you don't repair the problems, you will repeat them
- Daily refresh your love
- Because the design is different the diagnosis will have to be also.
- Sometimes your biggest hurt is really your biggest help
- Unconditional love is the only love that will survive in this relationship

Thank you, for reading. May God bless you and your relationship.
JUST MAKE SURE IT IS A RELATIONSHIP AND NOT A RELATION TRAP.

A Prayer For Our Couples

Dear father, I take this opportunity to pray for every couple individually and collectively. I pray for enlightment that leads to agreement. It is this agreement that leads to unification. Please open their eyes to understanding, wisdom and knowledge. I pray that individuality does not hinder or tear down the equality or the identity of their relationship. I pray for consciousness, and alertness that detects and discern all demonic attacks. That significance and agreement binds all evil influences.

That the power of your presence grant what is necessary for the success of their relationship. I pray for stability, Viability, and validity that secure this relationship's endurance. Lastly, I pray that their spirit is connected, and directed by you, in you and through you.

That the survival; is not intercepted by dictatorship. That forgiveness flourishes, and unconditional love resides. Give them Father, a peace that surpasses all understanding, and joy that is unspeakable. Now I ask that your hand rest on them, and your sweet communion of your Holy Spirit rule in them, and grant them many years of togetherness. Amen.

PRAYER FOR OUR SINGLES

Dear Father, I pray now for our singles. I pray that decision-making is led by the guidance of your Holy Spirit, and not deluded understanding. That desires, are not designed by impatience, and through frustration. That the realization of their identity; will not be overtaken by the influences of the enemy. Thank you, for wonderfully, and beautifully creating them. That past experiences does not dictate future endeavors. I declare wholeness, fullness, over their lives, fruitfulness, peace and unspeakable joy. I pray that every trap, and trick designed to demolish this single life is now met with the resistance of a renewed mind. I pray that any, and all modifications, reflections, and productive decisions are made prior to any pursuit. That the selections made are not anxious, nor fearful. I pray, that they would maintain competence; and use discretion.

Thank you, for the reassurance of being with them always, even to the end.

I pray, that in getting; let them secure understanding. In all their ways let them acknowledge you, and you will direct their paths. Let them find commonality, compatibility, and gain the capacity to acknowledge clarity. Allow your patience to do a mature work in their single lives. I pray for introspection, clear perspectives, and re-defined priorities in their lives.

Now Father, let you hand rest on them.

Thank you, for soothing doubts, calming fears, for the release of patience, the re-dedication to self-worth- a renewed strength- a revival of joy. Let the sweet communion of the Holy Spirit rest on them, rule in them, and with them. Amen.

PRAYER FOR OUR DIVORCEES

Dear Father, I pray now for all our divorcees.

I pray for all memory and history that may hunt, hurt, and taunt their peace. That the evidence of yesterday's pain, will not numb them to your presence and power in their lives. That the reality: does not dictate their revival. That your promise: to keep them in perfect peace, stands true in their life. Thank you, that through it all they gain strength. I pray, for an unspeakable joy, and an undeniable peace.

I pray for the capacity to forgive, even the unthinkable. I pray for the ability to trust again. Thank you, for the acceleration and momentum pass the agony.

Allow them to feel the warmth of you presence and your power. Thank you, for your word. That no weapon formed against them shall prosper.

Thank you, for my brother and my sister:

Breath of fresh air

New beginnings

A spirit of laughter again

Revived heart

Renewed mind

Redirection of self-worth

I pray that their memory becomes their momentum, and their history their hurdle.

Father, help them to accept what has happened for the bad, but to expect what is happening for the good. I do declare everything that has occurred is now working for their good. I declare, "The best is yet to come." Their eyes have not seen, their ears have not entertained the greatness that awaits them. Grant them the capacity to let it go...

Through the hurt, pain, lost, doubt, fear, bitterness, and memory, I declare wholeness after the brokenness.

Thank you, for working on them, through them and for them. If you be for them, who can be against them. Thank you, for the new smile, the new start, and the new self.

Now may your hand be on them. Let the sweet communion of your Holy Spirit rest, rule and abide with them. Thank you for their revival and their return. Amen

WARNING!!!
TO ALL COUPLES, BEWARE OF
DISTRACTIONS...
IF THEY CAN PAUSE YOU FOR A MINUTE, THEY
CAN STOP YOUR RELATIONSHIP FOR A
Lifetime...

ABOUT THE AUTHOR

Author – Elder Tim Grier native from Charlotte N.C married to Angier Grier has 5 children and 7 Grandchildren. He is assistant Pastor to Bishop Kevin L. Long at Temple Church International also serves as the Youth Pastor. A business man, manager, counselor, life coach. He believes: that if any man be in Christ he is new, and old things are passed away. He also challenges individuals to give their best in all that they do. You can reach out to him: ELDER Tim Grier Facebook- or timgrier0614@yahoo.com for questions or comments. For counseling, seminars, engagements

STAYING TOO
LATE
LEAVING TOO
SOON
TRICKS ✣ TRAPS ✣ TRUTHS OF RELATIONSHIPS
TIM GRIER

Is there a book inside of you? Ever wanted to self publish but didn't know how? Concerned about the financial part of self publishing? Relax. Take a deep breath. We can help!

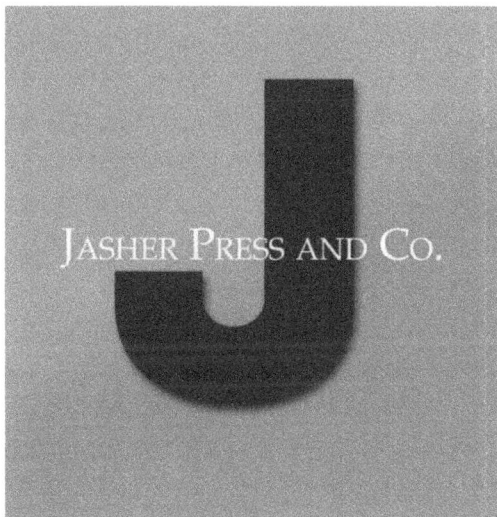

Finally! An affordable Self Publishing company for all of your Self Publishing needs. We have the right services, with the right prices with the right quality. So, what are you waiting for?

Unpack those dreams, break out that pen, your dreams of getting published may not be so far off after all!

Jasher Press & Co. is here to provide you with Consulting, Book Formatting, Cover Designs, editing services but most importantly inspiration to bring your dreams to past.

And this whole process can be done in less than 90 days! You thought about it, you talked about it but now is the time!

WWW.JASHERPRESS.COM
1-888-220-2068
CUSTOMERSERVICE@JASHERPRESS.COM

www.ingramcontent.com/pod-product-compliance
Lightning Source LLC
Chambersburg PA
CBHW060023100426
42740CB00010B/1572